NEW THEORY
OF
GRAVITATION

[BASED ON FUNDAMENTAL THEORY OF SINGULARITY – FTS]

Author: Prabhakaran Natesan

SHANATCO PUBLISHING

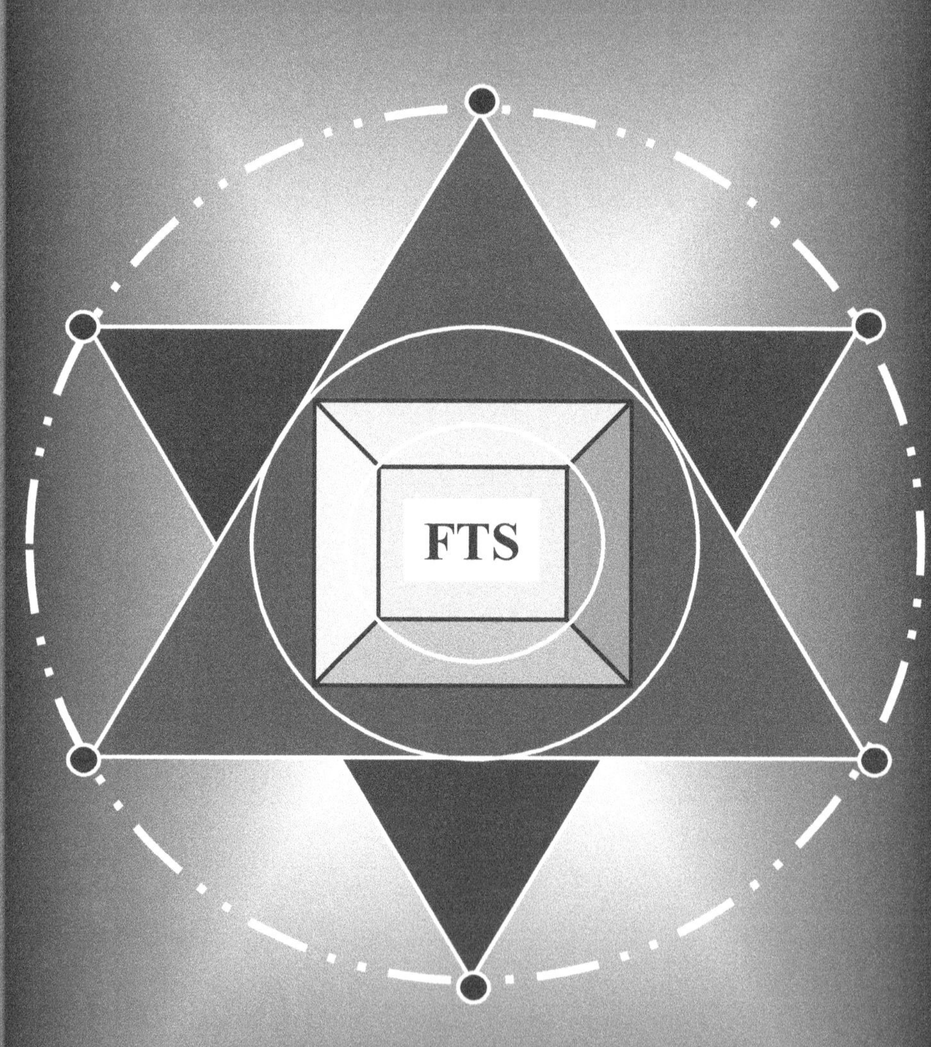
FTS

Self-published by **Shanatco Publishing**

Home Address: 63B, Kattabomman Street, Sri Karumariamman Nagar Extn, Perumattunallur, Chengalpattu District, Tamil Nadu, India. Pin code – 603202. Email: [shanatcop@gmail.com]

Purpose: Contribute for worldwide education

Pages: 123

Year of Publication – 2025

Copyright © Prabhakaran Natesan 2025

The ideas, techniques, drawings and explanations expressed in this book are author's own imagination and perspective.

PREFACE

Gravitation in reality, is a channel that has a dual face to conduct an up-streaming force from the source (Singularity) for creation of objects and a down streaming force for the objects to free fall and try to settle down with the deepest possible point in the Sp-ti medium at surface level but leads to destruction of objects near or open to the destination (Singularity). It is done through a single impeller mechanism at the depth of the medium which is same like a fan that draws the air from one side and pushes the same on the other side. Here the terms, upstream and downstream shall not be compared to the flow of a river, as it actually means pushing and pulling forces, away and towards the source-destination points respectively. Here the source point is same as the destination point at the depth of the medium called as "Singularity" and denoted as space zero time zero or simply Sp-ti 0. Now even if, Gravitation is understood in terms of gravity, it is still not a force at any point in the medium. This is because gravity is a resulting effect (felt with the masses) of this impeller, whose primary action force is to serve the purpose of driving the space-time medium itself in a cyclic manner and perhaps could be responsible for expansion and contraction of the Universe along with the mass-energy of the objects as well. Gravitation is independent of mass and fundamentally works with sp-ti 0 points governed by real dimensions. However, mass is dependent on gravitation for its creation and existence. At quantum level, particles float on Sp-ti waves and the thread of gravitation passes in the middle of the wave. The particle has to cross through the sp-ti 0s along this line which is called as sp-ti 0 axis or line of gravitation. Now, speaking to the point, free flow of the medium is restricted by some means and allowed only through channels, resulting in suction and driving forces in the space-time medium. This book also clarifies how in existing studies, the black holes are believed to have high gravity in it, is not true but the line of gravitation actually terminates at the edge and gravity is absolutely zero inside a black hole.

NEW THEORY OF GRAVITATION

1.0 FTS - BASIC INTRODUCTION

Gravitation is thought to be i) an invisible force, ii) a field of curved lines caused by heavy objects in space-time at macro-scale, iii) as an effect such as a free fall of an apple towards the ground or a moon revolving around the planet due to such curvatures and so on however, it is never imagined to be a channel to conduct a flow. We will begin the study from the idea of surface & depth of space-time medium and then to theory of gravitation. An ultimate discovery of space-time is introduced in this book which is the liquid nature of space-time hereafter referred to as **Sp-ti ocean**.

Where is this ocean situated in the Universe? Who has seen it before or is it even possible to reach there? According to Fundamental Theory of Singularity (FTS), the book published in the year 2024, based on the ideas discussed in it, when we zoom into the micro or nano scale to see the atoms and sub-atomic particles, we are not actually accessing the region of those objects in the existence and only the picture is enlarged. Then what would happen if we could reach the quantum scale? We would realize, quantum does not mean to be small, the objects appear same as in the macro world on reaching to this point or region. Means we are not really moving in the path towards the quantum region but simply stay in the macro-world to see quantum world to be smaller on comparison basis. It might sound weird but true. Even though it is not possible to physically reach to the quantum universe, the perspective could be sent through the path to visualize the reality.

The depth is mutual between the so-called macro and quantum worlds in terms of dimensions. To understand this, we shall imagine that as long as we are in the ground, the Earth appears flat however when we are away from the Earth and view it from space, it appears as a sphere. If we keep moving farther and farther away, the size of the planet appears smaller and smaller, becomes a dot and then completely vanishes from the sight. By this way of travelling, one could see the telescopic depth. Now, there is another type called microscopic depth in which the observing particle is already in a depth whose picture is brought closer to the sight using lens. This could be compared to that of travelling from far away distance towards the objects that appeared as a dot and grows in size by approaching closer and closer. However, in both the cases, the depth of the medium is observed but not accessed. We shall come across all these ideas in detail along with real dimensions of space-time. All the technical drawings and explanations in this book are new to studies and the ideas based on FTS solves the problems of theoretical physics in singular perspective, to be noted.

2.0 SURFACE AND DEPTH OF SP-TI MEDIUM - FTS

The foremost idea to be discussed is the depth of the medium. The existing study knows the Universe to be open with a same surface level everywhere in which Sir Einstein discovered that space and time are two different manifestations of the same thing to be called as **spacetime**. This single entity behaves as a fabric and thus bends for heavenly objects such as moon, planets, sun and stars due to their mass densities. The fabric and the curvature caused in it could be simply assumed for space, what is the significance of time to be considered here? This is because of the Einstein's experimentation with speed of light resulted in an observation called as **time dilation**. Later on, time dilation is said to be observed with gravitation too. Based on theory of relativity time dilation due to speed of light means travelling at the speed of light results in slowing down of the clock or the clock ticks slowly and attains time zero. Whereas, time dilation due to gravity means, when the clock is near to the heavy object it slows down and thus for high gravity as in case of black holes, the time stops ticking and becomes zero. Now, without involving relativity, we visualize time dilation based on FTS. Note that singularity and relativity (duality) are two opposite perspectives.

The first thing about time dilation is, it is a dual observation whose counter part is the **Length contraction**. We shall analyze the above said dual observation with the experimentation of speed of light. Before moving onto new theory of gravitation, we shall go through some topics in FTS to recollect the overall idea.

3.0 SPEED OF LIGHT – BASED ON FTS

Travelling of light has the ultimate speed limit of the Universe that nothing can travel faster than light. The speed of light in vacuum is measured to be 3 x 10^8 m/s.

We know the formula,

$$\text{Speed} = \frac{\text{Distance travelled (Km)}}{\text{Time taken (Hr)}}$$

Here, the distance is a fixed one. For example, a vehicle travelling at the speed of 60 Km/hr means the distance of 60 Km to be reached in one hour time, if uniform speed is maintained. Change in speed to be slow or fast, results in change in estimated time. So, the speed and the time are varying factors depending upon conditions. However, for a constant speed again, time is a fixed value to calculate. Now, what is happening with speed of light?

The same formula is applicable even for light but strange variations were observed that, there was a delay in time over the estimated time. As per the formula, time cannot change for a constant speed. Thus, the variation is accounted as dilation in time instead of **time-delay** which means same calculated time is assumed to have slowed down with slow ticking of clock.

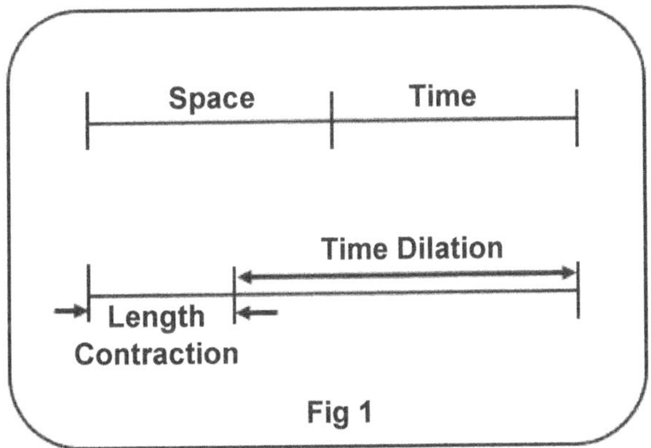

Fig 1

Let us consider space and time to be a line. Even though these two aspects are inseparable, to observe the variations we equally divide the line into two halves. Here, the change in one observation has obvious change in the other, constituting a dual observation. According to relativity, time dilation means slowing down of clock which is about measure of time. However, FTS utilizes the time in terms of line itself. A line with its length is associated with space, how come it could be used for time? Nobody knows what is meant by time in nature and here we assumed one half of the line to represent time and its variation due to speed of light as an extended line which in turn contracts the estimated length.

Here, length contraction directly means space to have contracted but what about time dilation? Even though the dilation seems to be extending, ticking of clock slows down towards a point that would cease to tick, means the time is reducing. Again, time here is not about a measure of clock-time but the above two aspects together shall be shown as a reduced scale imagined as follows,

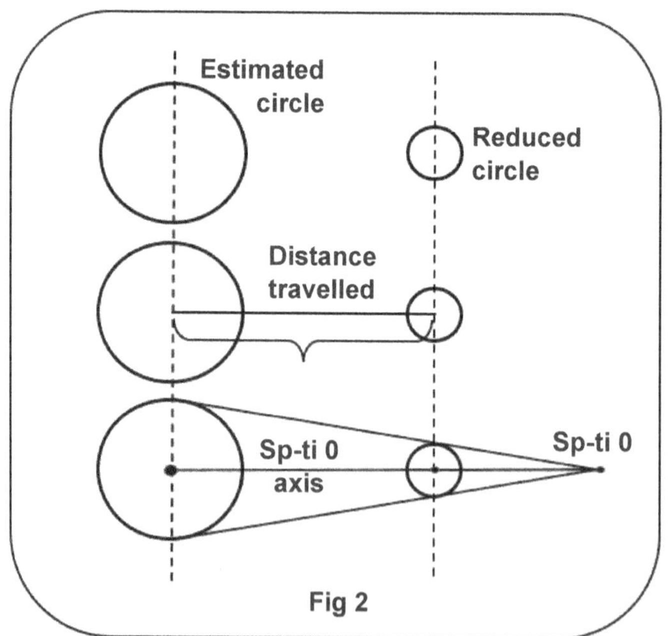

Fig 2

Fig 2 shows,

a) An estimated circle of space and time by us and there is a reduced circle representing the actuals in terms of length contraction and time reduction.

b) The reduced circle is shown at a distance from estimated one which means that, the variations are observed only with the speed of light photon that has travelled a distance.

c) The tangents drawn to touch the two circles are extended to meet at a point called **Sp-ti 0**. Thus, the axis connecting the three center points is called as **Sp-ti 0 axis**.

d) These two tangents also represent the value of length contraction and time dilation which were assumed to be continuous to reach space zero and time zero respectively for speed of light.

e) Further, the object travelling at the speed of light would achieve time zero which implies travelling faster than light would enter time negative, enabling us for time travel back in time.

f) With this, even twin theory was imagined that, twin siblings one living on earth and the other allowed to travel in space at the speed of light, on his return sees his brother on earth have grown older while he finds himself remain younger.

g) It implies, that the person travelled at light speed have now entered into the future on earth, where several years would have been passed relative to his travel in space only for a while.

h) Entering into the past is not believed based on the paradox that a grandson travelling to the past, if kills his grandfather then there is no possibility for him to take birth and live now at the present. Moreover, there is nobody showed up from the future to the present world, so travelling back in time is said to be impossible.

All the above assumptions according to relativity needs rectification with the visualization based on FTS,

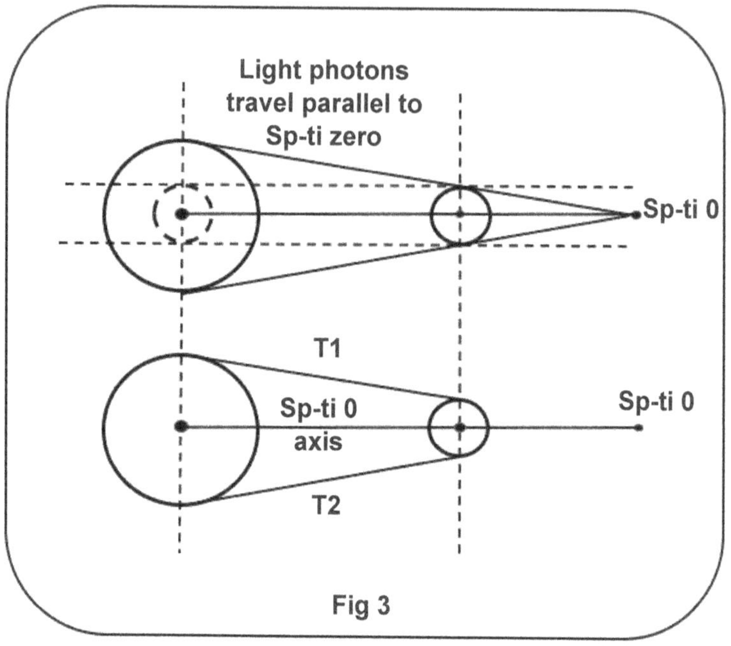

Fig 3 denotes the following points,

i) The light photons even without having to travel a distance with its speed, it is near to Sp-ti 0 with its volume.

ii) Therefore, the speed of light is never approaching zero and it is running parallel to Sp-ti 0 axis. The very photon is almost near to space zero with its volume.

iii) Here, space zero is same as time zero in a single point, as space-time was discovered to be a single entity, to be remembered.

iv) The diagram also shows the tangents T1 and T2 to have solved and not reaching Sp-ti 0, which means length contraction and time dilation observed with the speed of light are finite values and never tending to zero.

v) For a constant speed value of light, the variations observed obviously must have fixed values. Further, the indication of length contraction and time dilation in reality shows light photon to exist at a reduced scale, at some depth of the Sp-ti medium.

How to locate or mark the above said estimated circle and reduced circle in space-time medium. And where does this point of Sp-ti 0 exist? Here, the estimated circle is pertaining to human perspective, numbers and calculations whereas the reduced circle is a hidden factor unknown in existing studies and projected in our new theory of singularity. What does the reduced space time scale indicate? Shall be understood with the following real-time illustration.

Consider a water well with symmetry that looks like a cylinder as shown in Fig 4. There are two identical circles on top and bottom of the well. When we look into the well from top, the bottom circle appears smaller and situated well within the top circle.

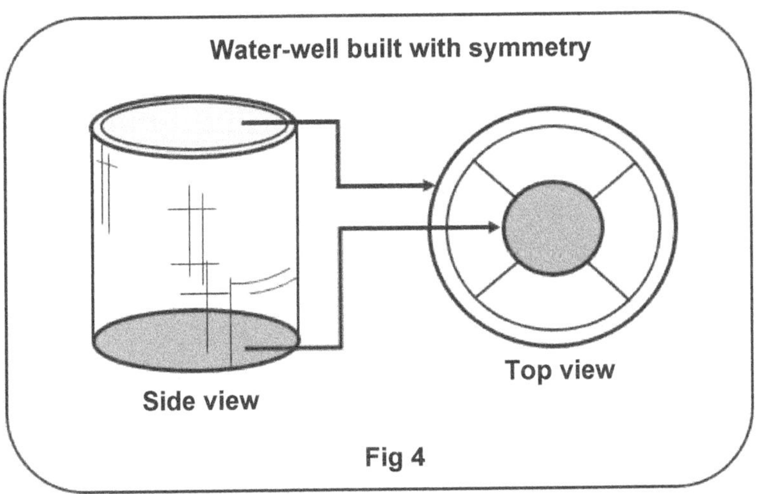

Fig 4

We know, this difference indicates the depth of the well. However, what do we mean by depth in our day-to-day life? It is a measurement made from top to bottom and vice versa is called as height. This way of understanding did not affect our calculations and technology in anyway. But depth is an important factor when it comes to space-time study. In reality we are not measuring the depth anywhere. It is only the height measured in two opposite ways.

Now, we are going to project the depth of the well, the way it appears. Let the two circles have the height difference but the depth is distinguished with different sizes of the circles as shown in Fig 5.

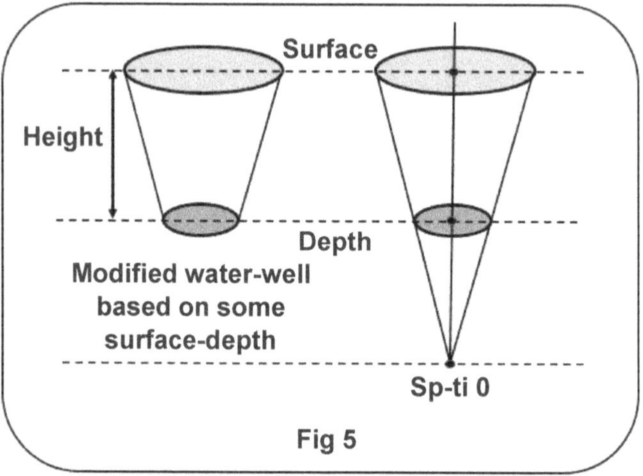

Fig 5

In Fig 5, height of the well is shown with double headed arrow such that measurement from top to bottom is not the depth. Moreover, depth has a duality of its own surface. If the depth of the well is further projected, it ends up with the point of Sp-ti 0.

From the discussions so far, we obtain a cone of depth leading to Sp-ti 0. If this Sp-ti 0 is the depth of space-time, then does it exist at the center of the Universe? The answer is no, first of all, the cone is not a fixed one. It is an appearance pertaining to the human vision. That means, the Sp-ti 0 is distributed throughout the Universe. Entire Sp-ti medium is made up of Sp-ti 0 points. The cone begins with a wide opening and ends with the apex point called Sp-ti 0 in any direction.

The reduced space-time scale means that space-time medium has surface and depth, where depth is not physically seen in any direction in the space we live. So, it requires diagrammatic representation to make a projection of the same for our understanding.

In case of water well, the depth is only a shadow such that, it is possible to reach the point of depth as it is constituting a deep appearance only. However, in case of light, it is really deep and travelling of photons happens in deeper space.

Thus, by applying cone of depth for light in space-time medium, the observations such as length contraction and time dilation are projected to the surface as shown in Fig 6.

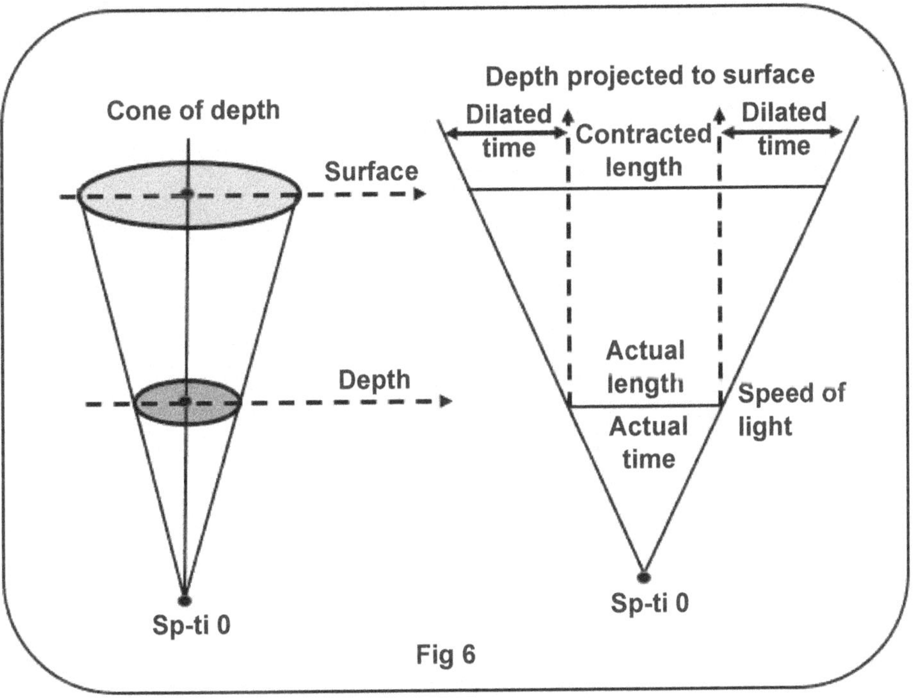

Fig 6

Moreover, the gap between estimated and reduced circles shown in Fig 2 is no more a distance but a depth. The representation of reduced circle actually contains length contraction and time dilation in terms of space contraction and time reduction in it, could be better understood in the fore coming topics.

Fig 6 shows the actual length by actual time of light at certain depth which is appearing as shortened or contracted length and measured as dilation in time respectively on the surface we live.

4.0 BENDING PATH OF LIGHT – BASED ON FTS

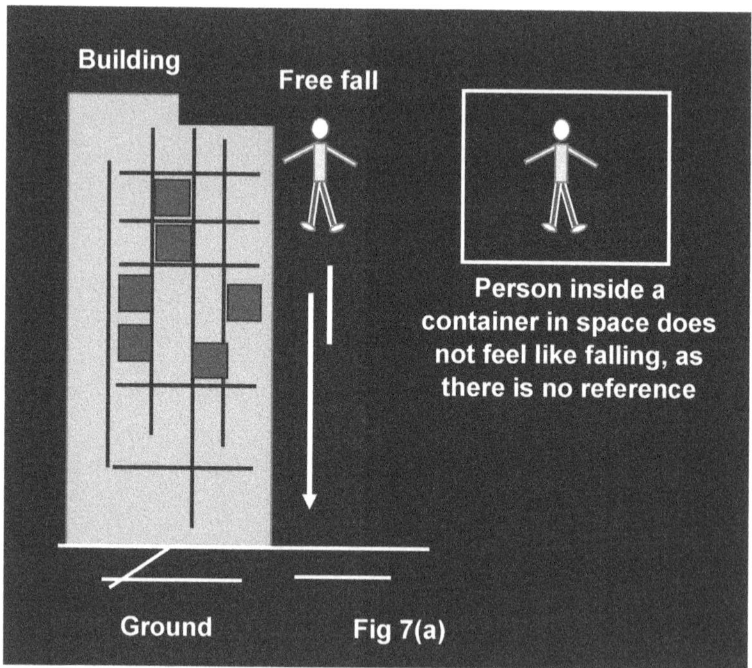

There is an idea of bending of light path along with the gravitational field, which could be understood with the real-time illustration (as in the existing studies). Fig 7(a) shows the person jump off a building feels his falling downward towards the ground. Whereas, in space the person inside a container moving down at a speed does not feel like falling, as there is no reference. However, in case of elevator, Fig 7(b) when its moves downwards with the minimum acceleration of 9.8 m/s^2 onwards the observer and a ball placed on the floor surface does not feel its weight.

Now, when the elevator moves in upward direction accelerated for the same situation, both observer and the object each experiences their own weight.

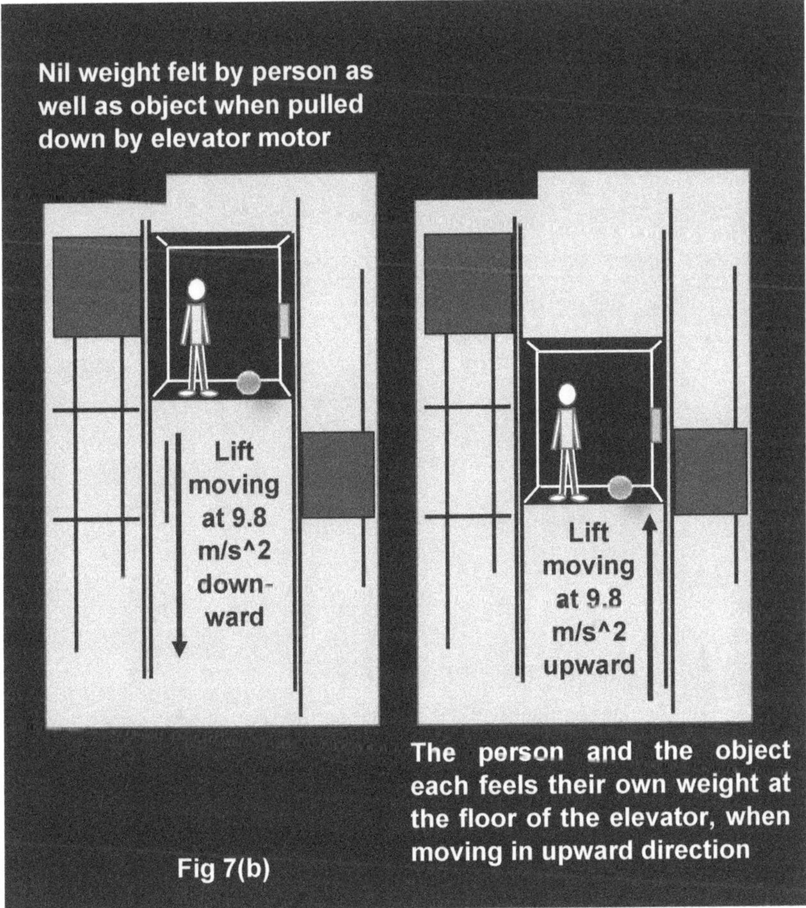

Consider, the ball is thrown by the observer to the wall, the path of the ball is straight when the lift is not moving however, when the lift is moving in upward direction the path of the ball bends as shown in Fig 8(a) and try to be with the ground for its stability based on local gravity. Same way, the light beam is imagined such that the straight-line path of the light bends with the gravity.

This phenomenon is verified by the scientists, based on the fact that gravitational field of Sun is greater than Earth, during a solar eclipse the Moon hides the Sun exactly to show only the shadow to be seen from the Earth. So, at this time, the picture of objects such as stars located far away from the sun on its other side, must be carried by the photons which bends along the curved space around the sun to reach the observer's telescope. The image of stars is captured at certain point proving Einstein's prediction of Space-time to behave like a fabric is true and so the curved gravitational field associated with the heavy objects.

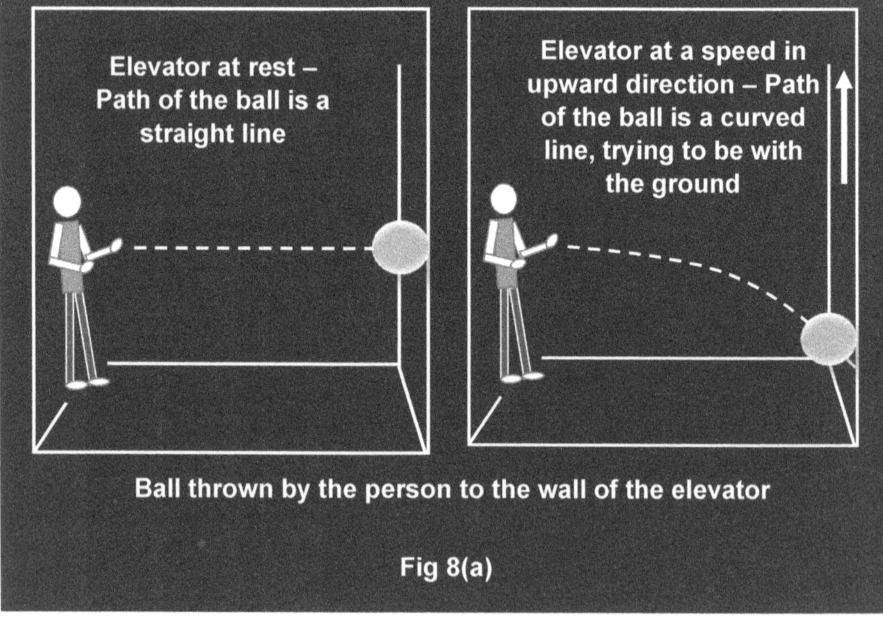

Fig 8(a)

Now, the path of bending light beam in case of elevator is not the same with bend in gravitational field which is assumed to be a curvature caused by heavy objects (not clearly differentiated in existing studies), to be noted.

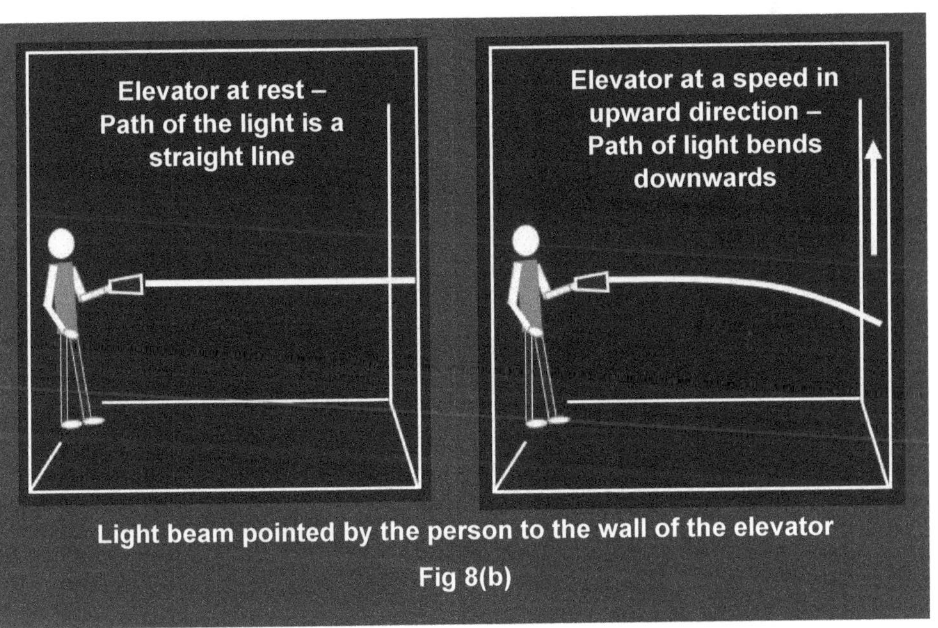

Light beam pointed by the person to the wall of the elevator

Fig 8(b)

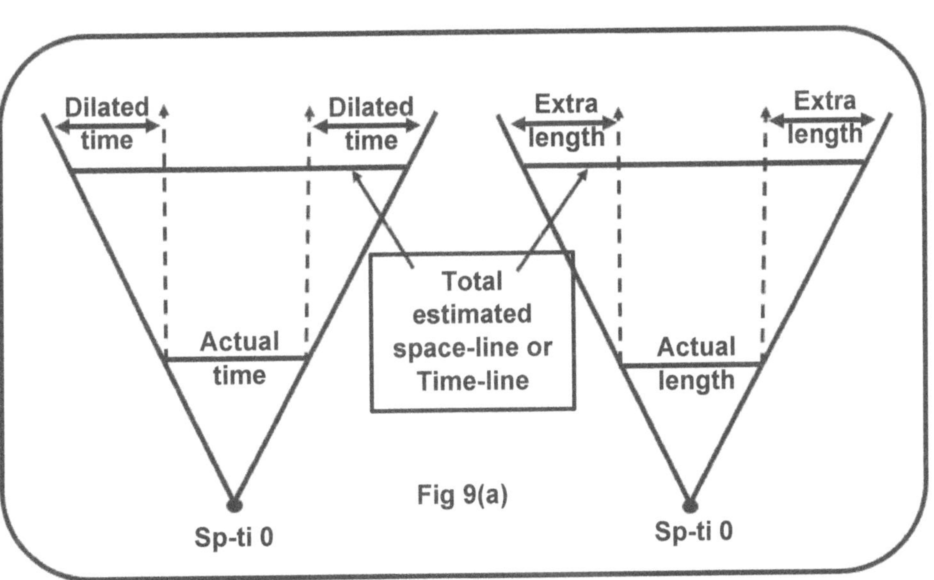

Fig 9(a)

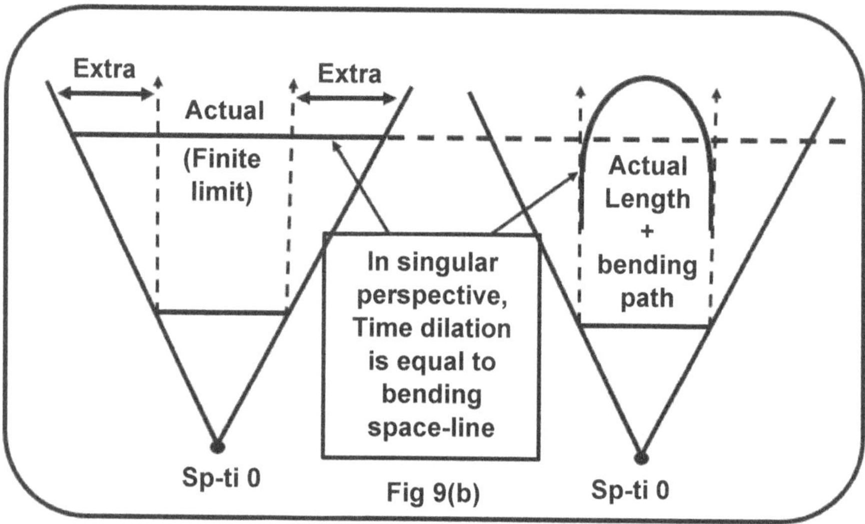

For clear understanding let us assume the speed of the elevator moving in upward direction is not accelerating at 9.8 m/s^2 but at the speed of the light itself. As we said the path of the light beam bends, then to what extent the path bends and the limit which the light curve does not exceed could be understood with the Fig 9(b).

Since we have introduced sp-ti frames, the bending must be traced with surface and depth of sp-ti medium for space as well as with the moving frames for time, together called as **Sp-ti frames**. The path of light beam observed within the elevator does not serve a complete thought experiment. It must be bent on either side and curve to be within limits as shown in Fig 9(c). This could be further clarified with moving light clock illustration in modern days in understanding time dilation. However, it is also a misconception but the idea is good and shall be utilized to understand length extension and actual time delay (topic follows) by applying singular perspective.

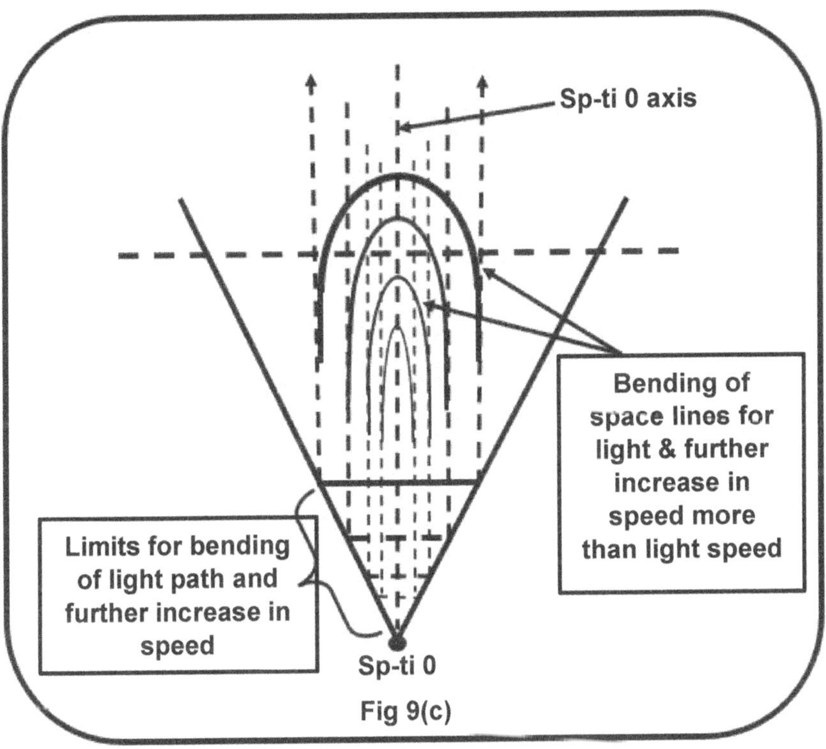

The bending of space lines for light speed and further increase in speed more than light speed are shown in Fig 9(c).

The actual curved length of light means the length of the light beam in one sp-ti frame for a moment whereas the bending curved path of light means how deep this actual length from surface to depth of sp-ti medium.

Time dilation = [Actual curved length of light + Bending path of light] From surface to depth

Time dilation = [Estimated length – Contracted length] Only at surface level

5.0 LENGTH EXTENSION AND ACTUAL TIME DELAY
(Light clock illustration) – BASED ON FTS

The path of light is said to be at the depth and the observer lives on the surface of Sp-ti medium, what is the impact when the light is experimented by the observer is the most important technique of analyzing space-time. We shall understand the same with the light clock, a method of understanding length contraction and time dilation. However, it is applied in the opposite way in favor of relativity. Let us see the illustration clearly.

Stationary light clock

**Actual length at the depth and
bending within limit**

Moving light clock

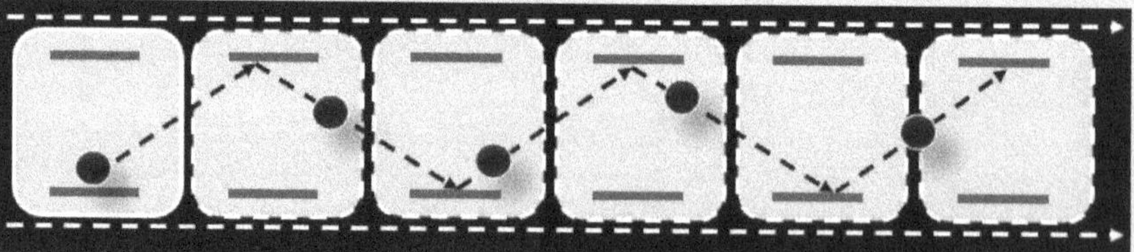

**Length extension on the surface of Sp-ti medium
however bending path at the depth is within limit**

Fig 10

The light clock is wrongly convincing for length extension instead of contraction and making actual time delay instead of time dilation. This could be cleared with v-diagram representation, Fig 11(a).

Here, besides the curved length of light at the depth, the bending of its path along the scale also to be noted. The speed more than the light speed causes more bending as well as thinning of lines towards the vertical Sp-ti 0 axis is shown. The limits for further increase in speed more that light is also shown to reduce to reach Sp-ti 0 point or axis, Fig 9(c).

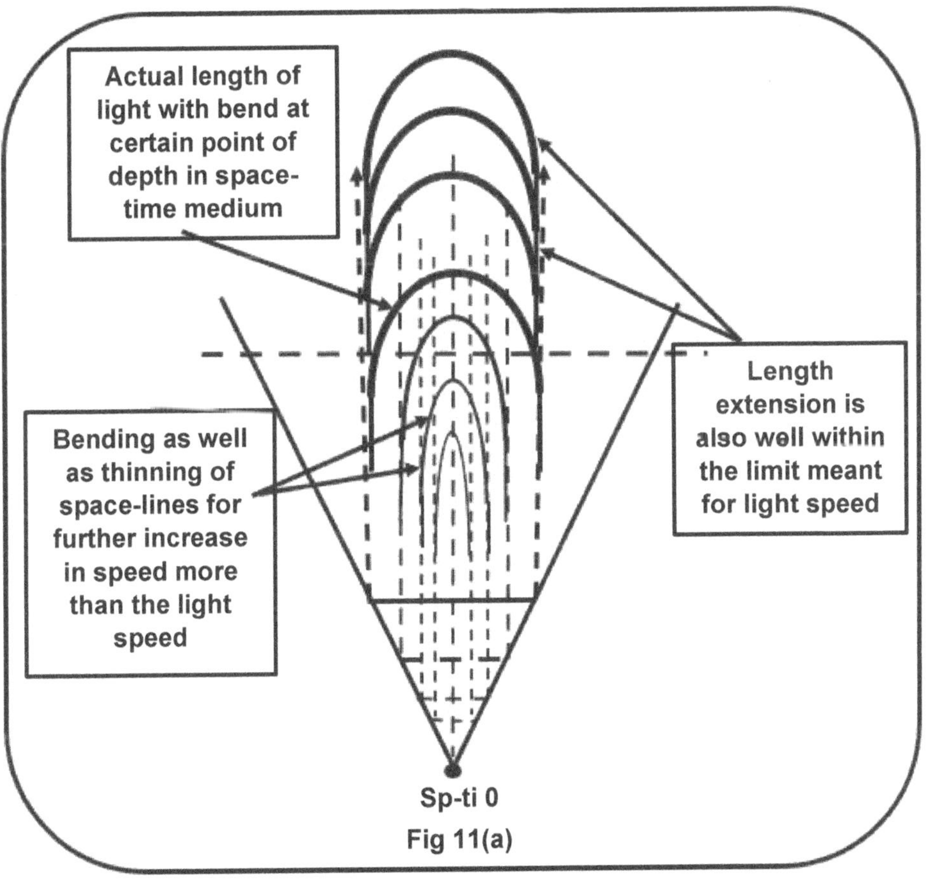

Fig 11(a)

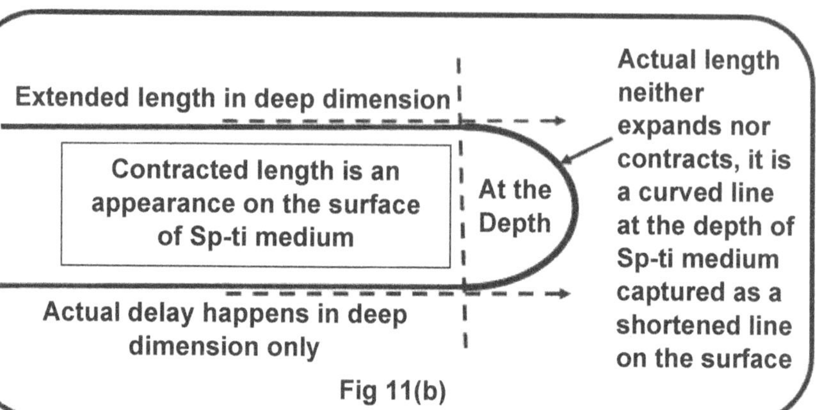

Fig 11(b)

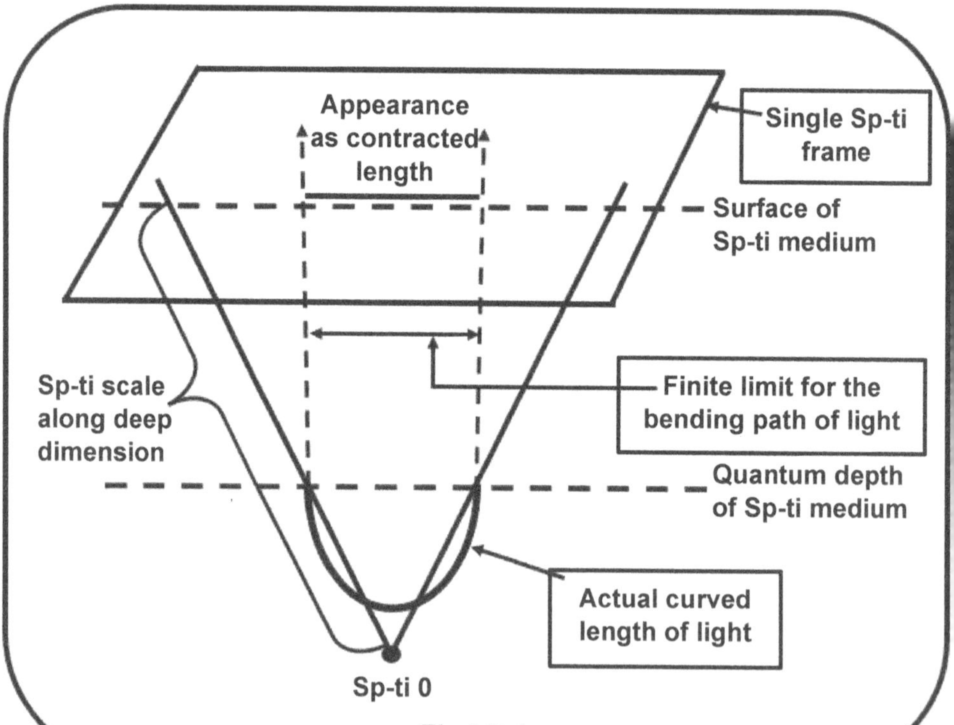

Fig 11(c)

Important note: Fig 11(c) shows, even for length extension more than the actual curved length of light happening in light-clock illustration, it is not visible in wide dimension, it happens radially along deep dimension. Only the shortened length appearance could be seen on the surface of sp-ti medium we live. The curved length of light is shown at the bottom in the representation so as to distinguish its quantum depth from the surface of the medium. However, we have already discussed that the real cone of depth is not physical but dimensional and only its shadow could be realized on the surface.

Space-time frame or Sp-ti frame:

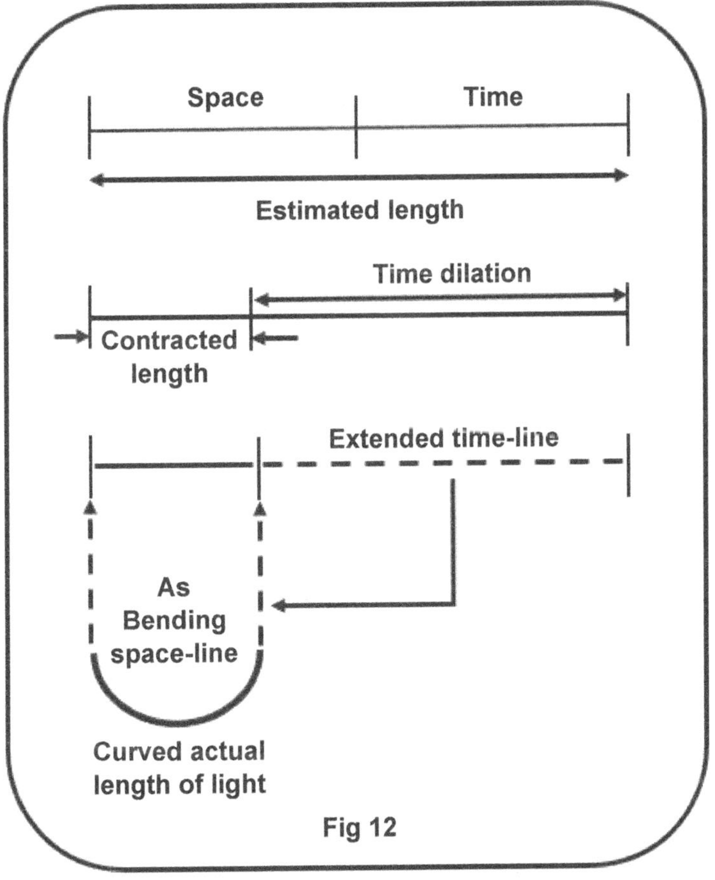

Fig 12

So, the time dilation is slowing down of time in relativity whereas FTS considers as a time-line into a bending space-line to represent the bending path of the light hidden behind for each contracted length at the surface which in turns indicates surface and depth difference in Sp-ti medium. Fig 13, shows a numerous breaklines as contracted lengths in the surface Sp-ti frame which are actually projected from the Sp-ti frame capturing one moment of light at the depth. This means that length contraction and time dilation eventhough observed only by experimenting the speed of light they are more fundamental than the speed factor. Now, if the Universe is still assumed for surface only then either the speed value determined for light must be true or the dual observation such as length contraction and time dilation must be true.

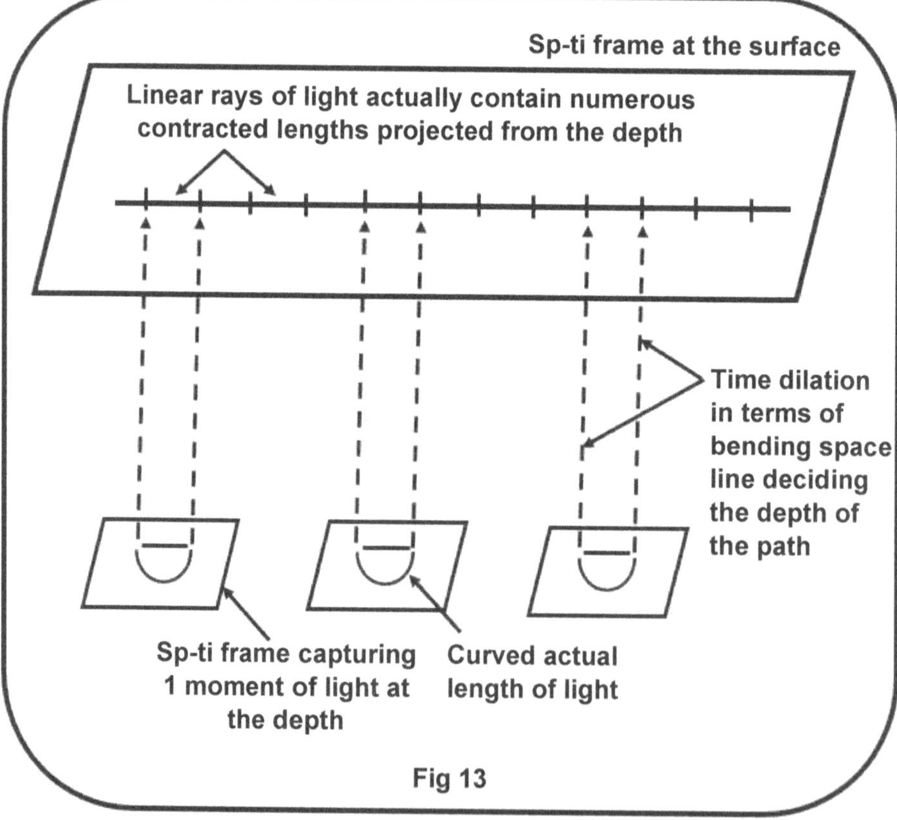

Fig 13

6.0 TIME DILATION DUE TO GRAVITATION - FTS

We know the gravitation in macro-scale by general theory of relativity. However, we make use of the idea to understand time dilation in singular perspective.

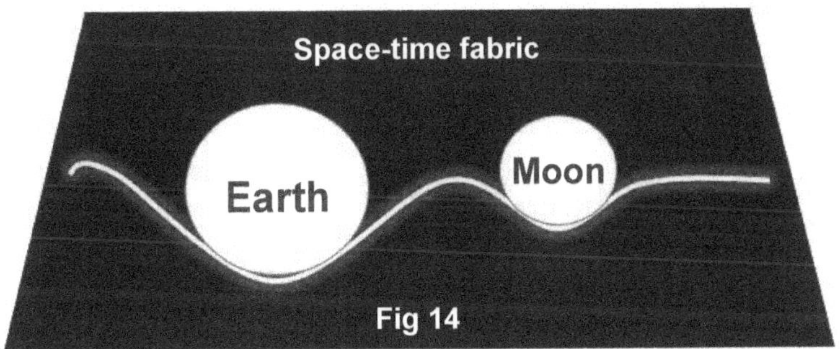

Fig 14

We see the curvature of single line caused by the object to appear like sagging in space-time fabric. However, with double line representation, it shows that the space-time fabric is actually bitten by the object. Also, the unbent double line means a flat space-time medium without heavy objects or in other words, the objects within this tolerance limit does not bend space-time grid lines of the medium. This dual line with certain limits could be termed as **"Sp-ti tolerance"** (to be discussed in detail in fore coming topics).

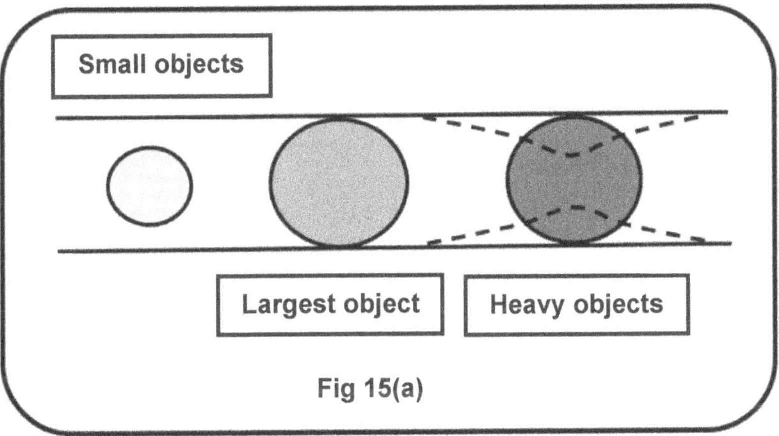

Fig 15(a)

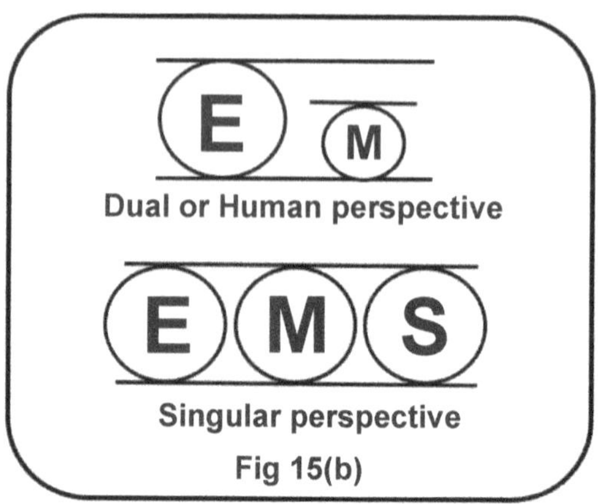

Now, for further analysis there is a crucial technique to be applied. We know the heavy objects such as Moon, Earth and Sun are in different sizes. Clearly, the bending of sp-ti lines of the medium is only due to the mass density of the object.

So, for our representation the size factor has no significance and could be eliminated such that all the objects are shown with circles of same size and the difference is indicated only with the amount of bending pertaining to their densities, Fig 15(c).

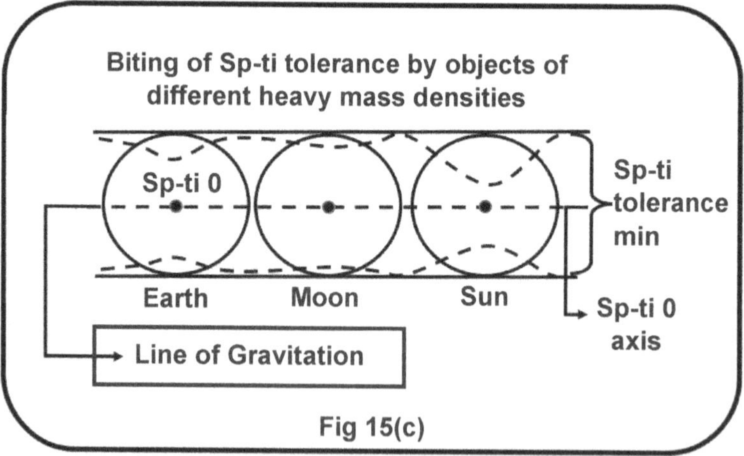

Fig 15(c) shows that the bending of sp-ti line differing with mass densities of Earth, Moon and Sun. This is the minimum point from where the Sp-ti tolerance starts reducing. To see the maximum limit of this Sp-ti tolerance, we need another way of representation [Fig 15(d)], so that it is possible to know the maximum utilization of the tolerance by certain object. Whereas black holes are beyond this limit.

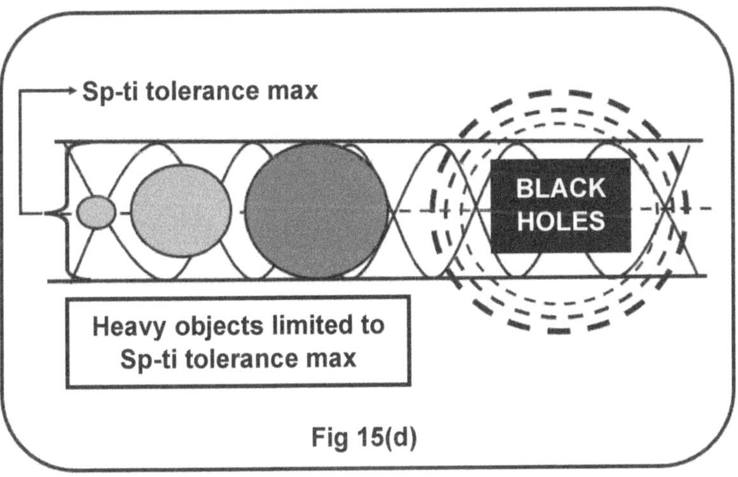

Fig 15(d)

Time dilation 1: Observed with variation (curvature caused) in Sp-ti tolerance max due to heavy objects. This bending of space-time line forms ridges. Thus, here the time dilation is the indication of surface and depth in terms of crests and troughs on the overall surface of the Sp-ti medium, Fig 16(a).

Time dilation 2: Observation made on the surface of space-time we live, which is actually a projection from the depth where the light is travelling, Fig 16(b). Thus, in this case time dilation is the indication of surface and depth of the entire space-time medium.

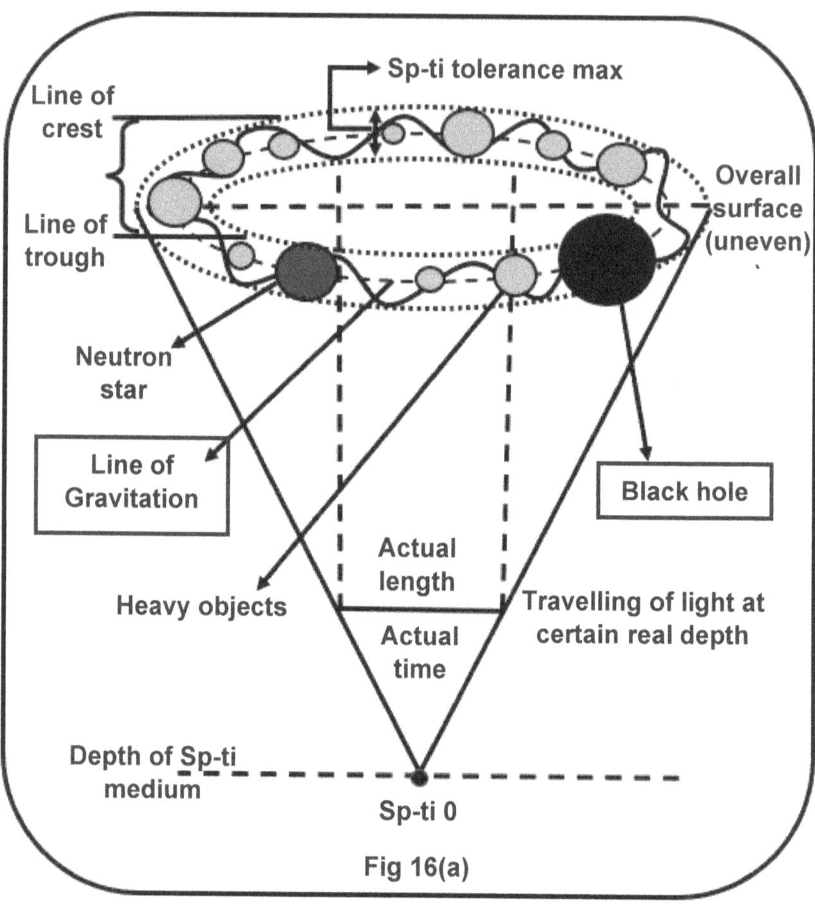

Fig 16(a)

Conclusion: In both the cases time dilation is accounted for difference in up & down and surface & depth levels. It shall not be imagined for time travel with relative speed which is a further significance while it has already served its purpose to indicate the depth of the medium and done with it. Now, it is up to the people to still believe time dilation could be applied for some time travel based on theory of relativity.

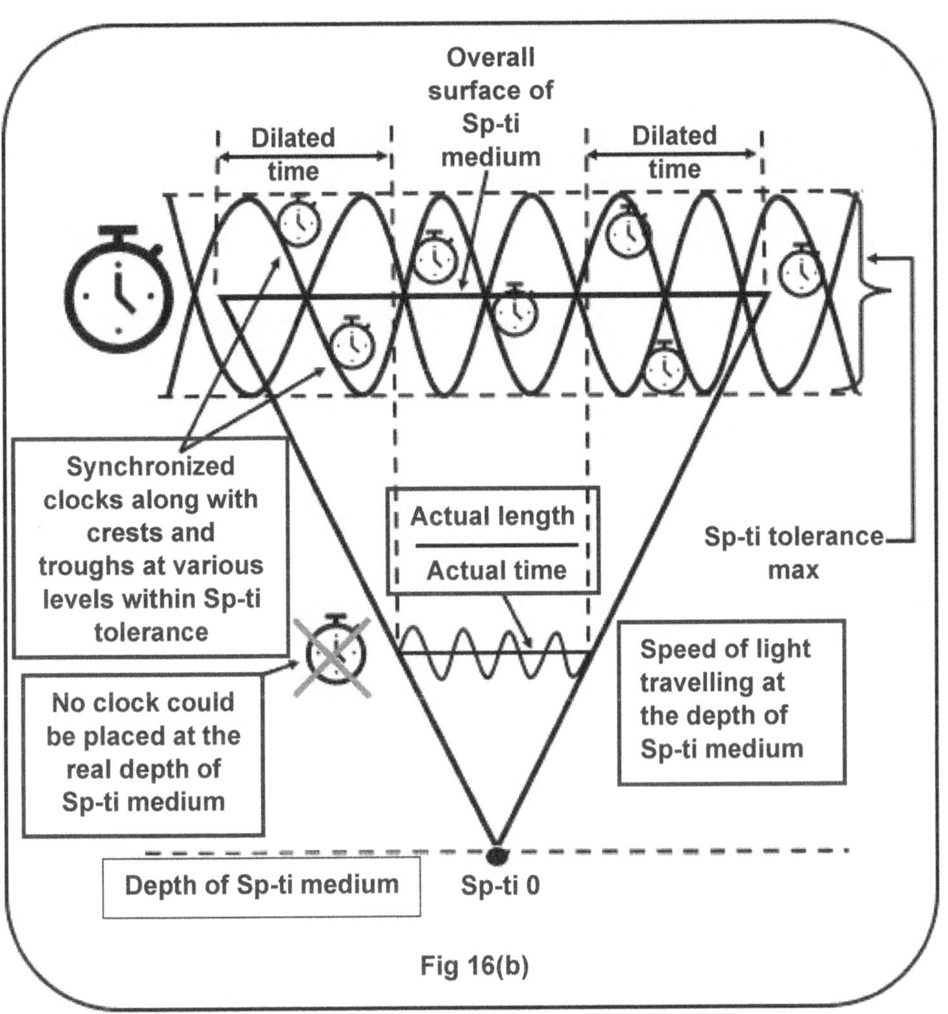

Fig 16(b)

V- Diagram Representation: Relativity and singularity have only one thing in common, it is the point that could be simply denoted by the English alphabet 'V'. In which way it is further derived leads to the two straight opposite understandings. However, relativity just remains a concept even though many of the ideas of Sir Einstein proved in recent studies. It is a very deep insight, missing of which relativity sounds absolutely right.

Evidently, relativity does not lead to quantum mechanics and controversial too. General theory of relativity (GR) is applicable only for macro-scale objects and quantum mechanics (QM) is another branch of physics to explain the nature of quantum-scale objects.

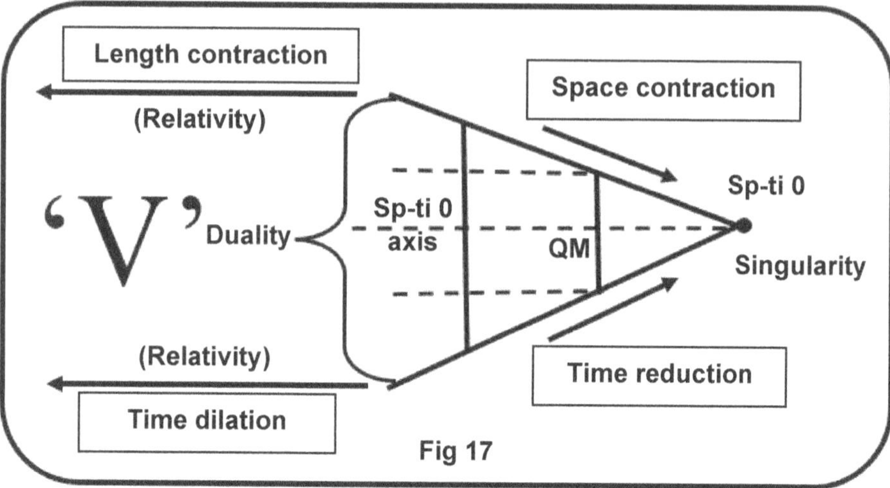

Fig 17

Relativity did not serve the fundamental theory of everything. The term relativity itself means a duality whose path fails to lead to singularity and projected in opposite direction indeed.

The concept of relativity is same like the threads that are twisted out would not be let into the loop hole of the needle to serve the purpose of stitching. The true findings such as length contraction and time dilation are dual observation in nature. One does not exist without the other and hence each one does not mean anything like instantaneous travelling with zero distance, moving back and forth in time etc. In short, theory of relativity is derived or understood in the way opposite to quantum mechanics and that is the reason for its contradiction. In reality, both the observations together reduce in a scale, pass through the quantum range and then to reach the point of **nothing** or the ultimate single deepest point of all Sp-ti 0s called as **Singularity.**

7.0 BLACK HOLES – BASED ON FTS

i) The force involved in a black hole is not gravity:

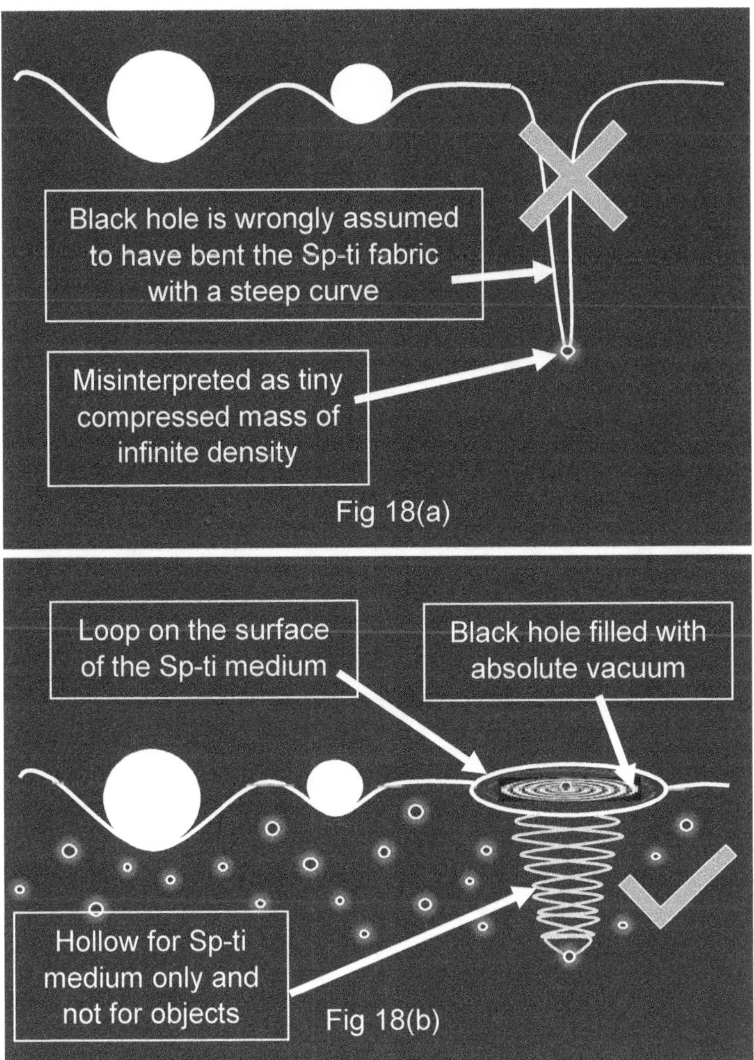

From FTS we have seen, the sp-ti grid and the line of gravitation terminates at the edge of the black hole. Then what is the destructive force inside a black hole that pulls the objects of the Universe? There is an impeller action at the depth of the sp-ti medium, whose mechanism is basically to drive the sp-ti medium in a cyclic manner. Besides this, the force is utilized for creation of objects pushed away from singularity and the resulting force is pulled by the other face of the same impeller that draws the objects or the medium itself towards singularity. Here, clearly the sp-ti lines are only bent by the objects and not by black hole is shown.

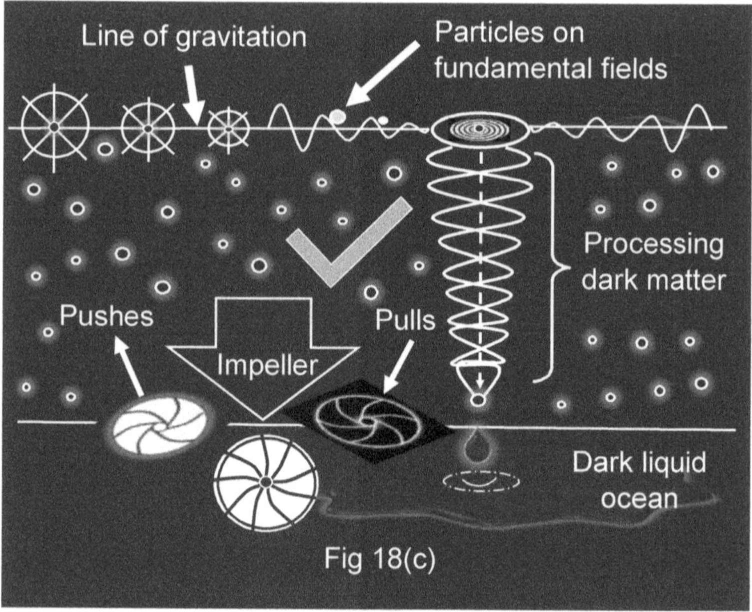

Fig 18(c)

The line of gravitation is the thread at the core of the gravitational rope from macro-scale to quantum scale and terminates at the edge of the black hole. The wave nature of the sp-ti medium is surrounding the black hole means how big the hole could be, it is defined to be deeper than quantum object as it has no space no time even for a fundamental particle. However, dimensionally Singularity is the deepest Sp-ti 0 of all.

We will discuss a simple idea about Sp-ti medium for its cyclic flow and the force behind it. Drinking the water from the glass tumbler directly by mouth is different from drawing the water with a straw. Same way, the flow of fluid medium is restricted by channels and thus, suction and driving forces are possible.

The force involved in a black hole is actually not pertaining to the black hole but just exposed through it, as the hole is open between surface and depth of the medium all along, to be understood. The gravitation has no connection with this force and the primary action of this impeller force is intended for driving the medium only.

ii) Nature of space-time medium:

To understand black holes better, we need to know the nature of space-time medium in which it is formed. It is the fluid nature that constitute the medium. We know fluid means both liquid and gaseous states of matter and let us consider this matter to be dark. Then, sp-ti ocean is basically a liquid form. There are two kinds of vacuum namely 1) Spacious vacuum and 2) Absolute vacuum. Now, visualizing the above points of fluidity as follows

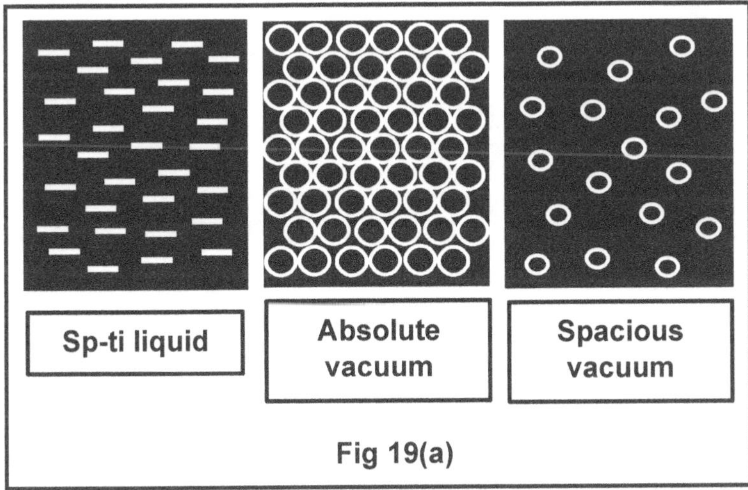

Here the absolute vacuum itself is in gaseous form however, the sp-ti 0s are close together and not suitable for the motion or even creation of objects. So, the Universe is actually existing in spacious vacuum. Absolute vacuum filled in a black hole means there is no entry for objects. An object obviously has to compress itself to occupy space-time zero point which means the object does not exist at this point.

Moreover, absolute vacuum serves as the insulation layer over the liquid Sp-ti medium and also has a layer coating continuing even to prevent the object leaking from within. This absolute vacuum is the fabric or membrane of sp-ti medium however, we know that only the heavy objects could realize or touch it. How to visualize the same?

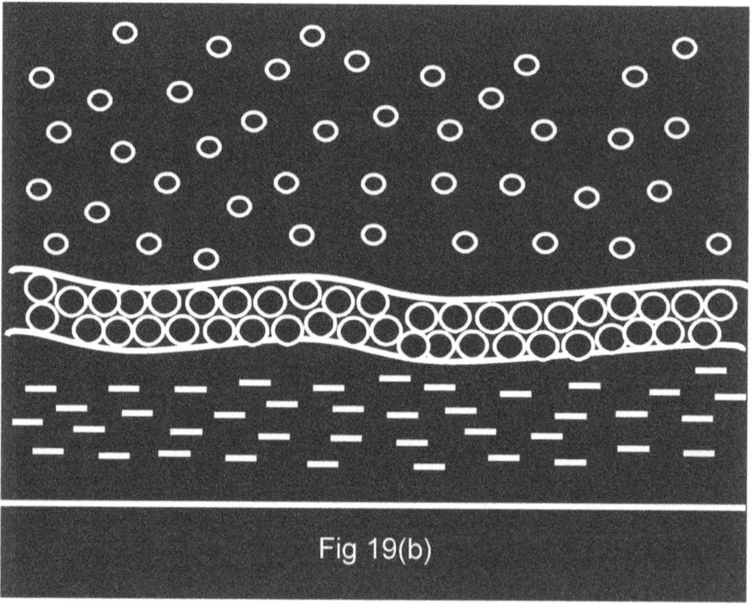

The three states of fluid nature are separated as in Fig 19(b) however, they are not identified in the medium as simple as this representation. It is based on real dimensions of space-time explained in FTS. Here, each point is called as Sp-ti 0 which in turn is a black hole. The object could be never thought of touching the liquid, as it becomes nothing even reaching at the edge of a big black hole. Whether a black hole is larger or smaller it behaves as a single point irrespective of its size.

iii) Structure of black holes and Sp-ti grid formation:

The space-time medium is flat everywhere and we see only the surface of the Sp-ti ocean (hidden dimensionally) that serves as the background of the Universe. There is no such a thing called as black hole in the existence. We are using the term as a continuation of existing study otherwise absolute vacuum is the appropriate scientific term to define such nature in reality. We will see the structure of a Sp-ti 0 as a point of creation and destruction each but has opposite faces.

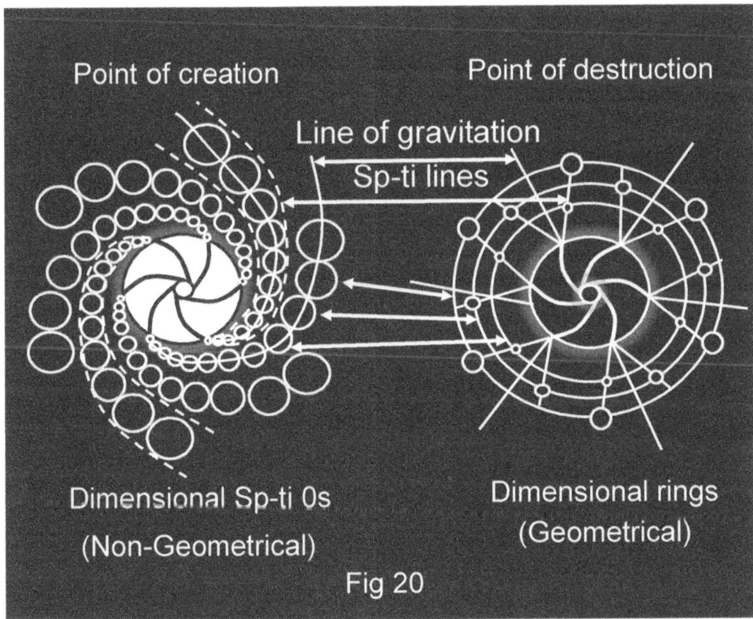

Geometrical and non-geometrical representations for creation and destruction points are vice versa and only the face difference to be noted. The alignment of Sp-ti 0s around the creation and destructions points are shown in Fig 20 where the dimensional Sp-ti 0s are same as the dimensional rings. Both the format will give rise to the Sp-ti grid lines. The point of creation is responsible for the sustainment of medium as well, which is differentiated as a point of light whereas the singularity of destruction is dark point as shown in Fig 22.

Sp-ti grid
line
Sp-ti grid line
Singularity
Sp-ti grid formation through non-geometrical aspect

Fig 21

Sp-ti 0 (Wide)
Sp-ti 0 (Deep)
Sp-ti 0 (Minute)
Sp-ti grid lines
Sp-ti 0
(Point of
generation)
Sp-ti 0
(Point of
absorption)
Dark liquid ocean
Sp-ti grid formation through geometrical aspect

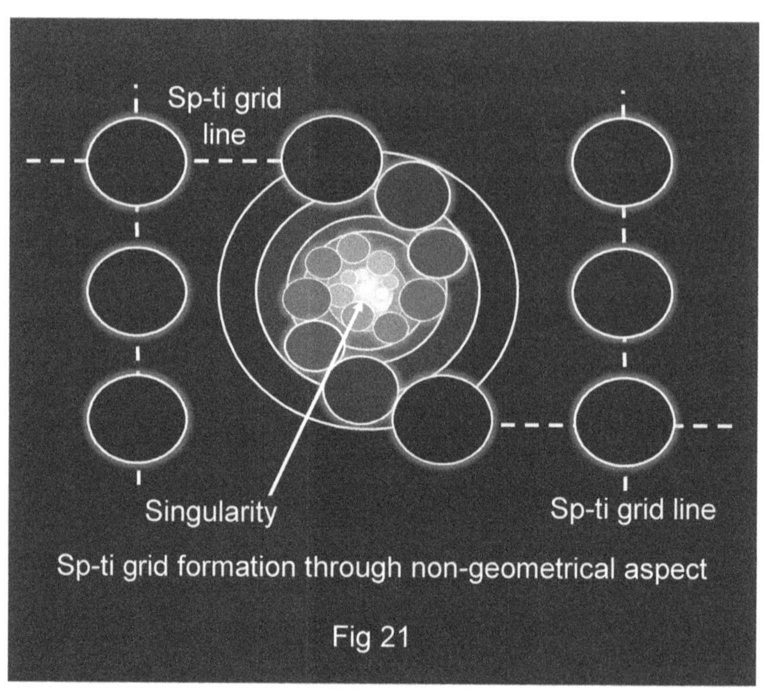

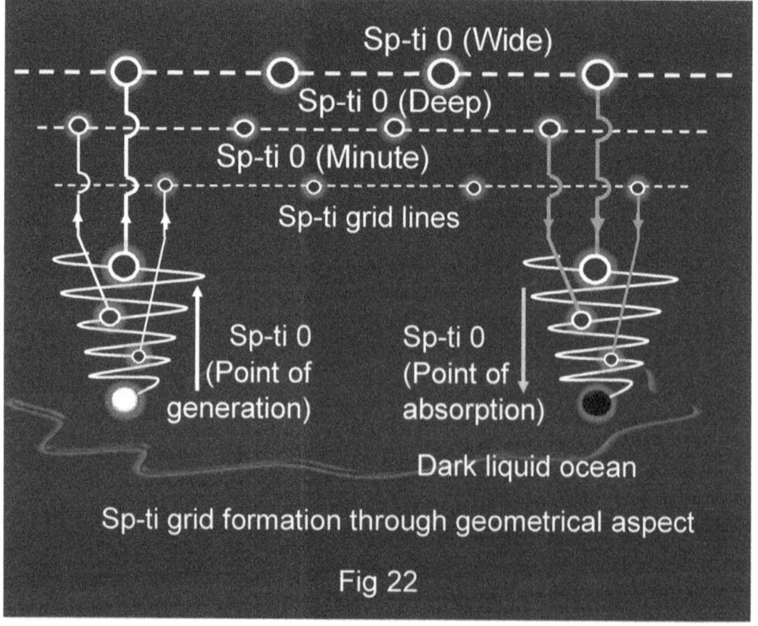

Fig 22

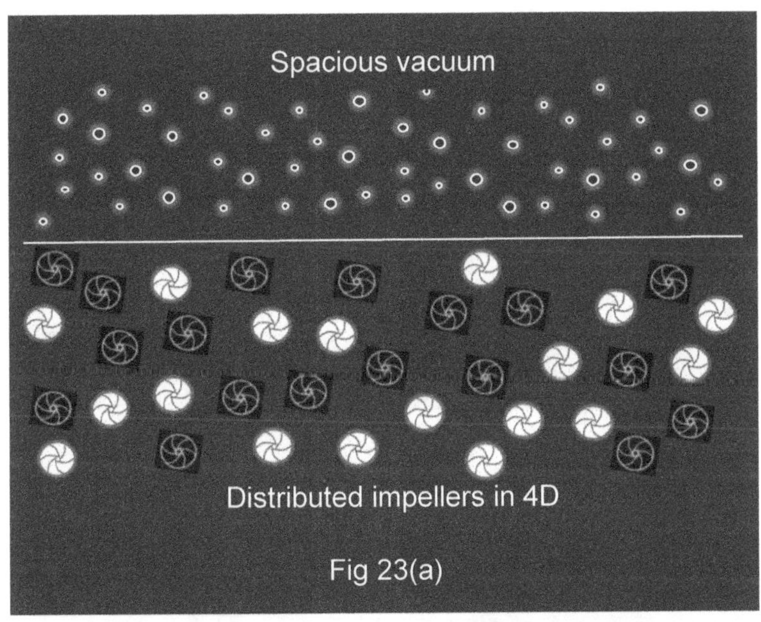

Spacious vacuum
Distributed impellers in 4D
Fig 23(a)

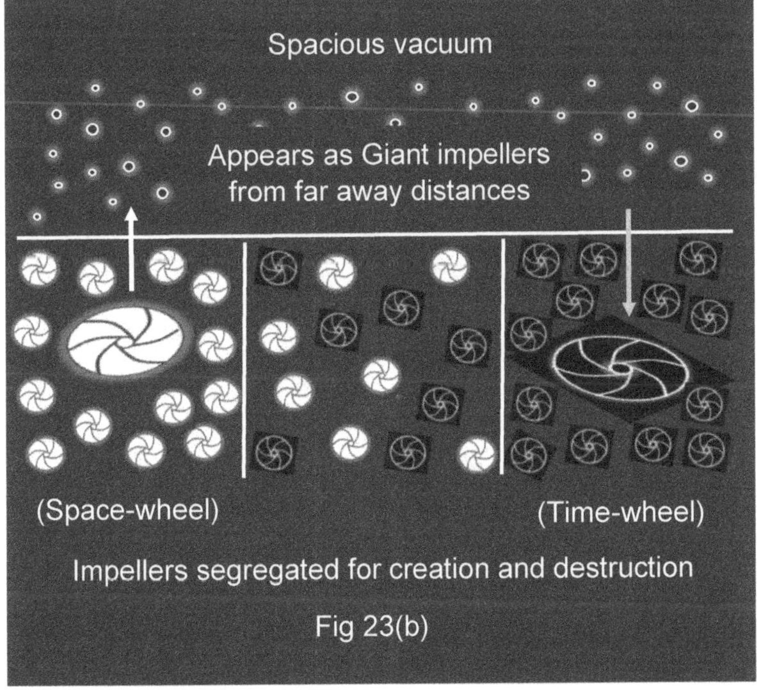

Spacious vacuum
Appears as Giant impellers
from far away distances
(Space-wheel)
(Time-wheel)
Impellers segregated for creation and destruction
Fig 23(b)

The impellers are present all over the existence, we shall consider the impellers of pushing face for both creation & sustainment of objects and driving the cyclic flow of the medium as well.

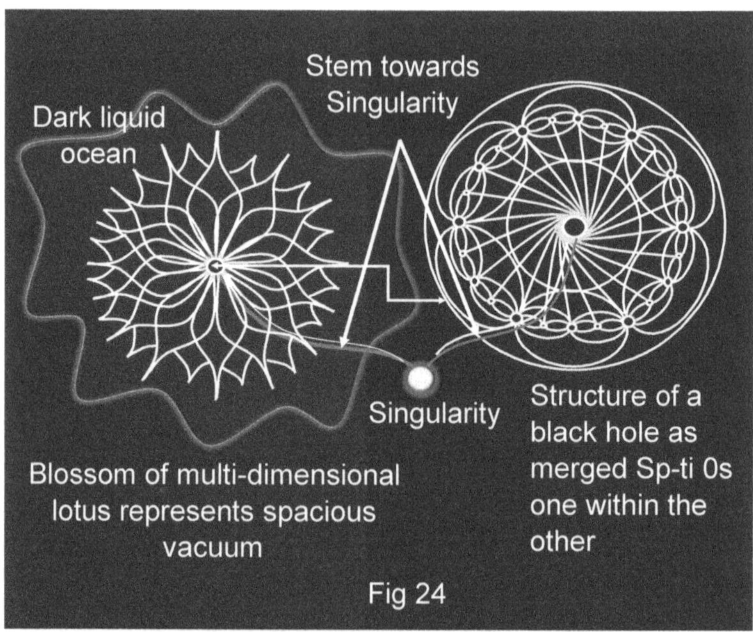

Fig 24

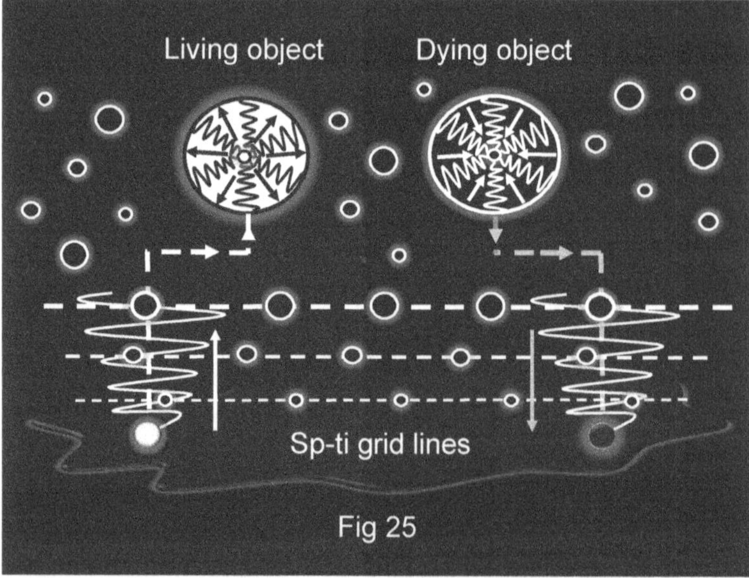

Fig 25

Sp-ti 0 points would settle down and merge one within the other (Fig 24) without these impellers. So, the impellers being active, causes the sp-ti grid formation which is common for both destruction and creation except for the direction of force towards or away from singularity. We call the destructive impeller to be the time-wheel, as it is always and everywhere available in the existence however, the force is met only at the final frame (dead end) of an object, as in case of a neutron star.

Let us consider the dying object to be a neutron star. The object reaches to a stage and ready to breakdown with pulling forces of destructive impellers. So, this self-destruction of an object to become a black hole is different from a black hole that destructs the other nearby objects. Means, the active stars collapsed by a black hole are actually not at the stage of self-breakdown but forced for destruction. Then what is happening out there. After a complete breakdown, the impellers continue to disturb the medium which causes the nearby objects to collapse. As discussed earlier, the object deforms into fields however, it is unlike the fundamental fields, floods like mingled-fields and drain through the sp-ti grid lines towards singularity as shown in Fig 26.

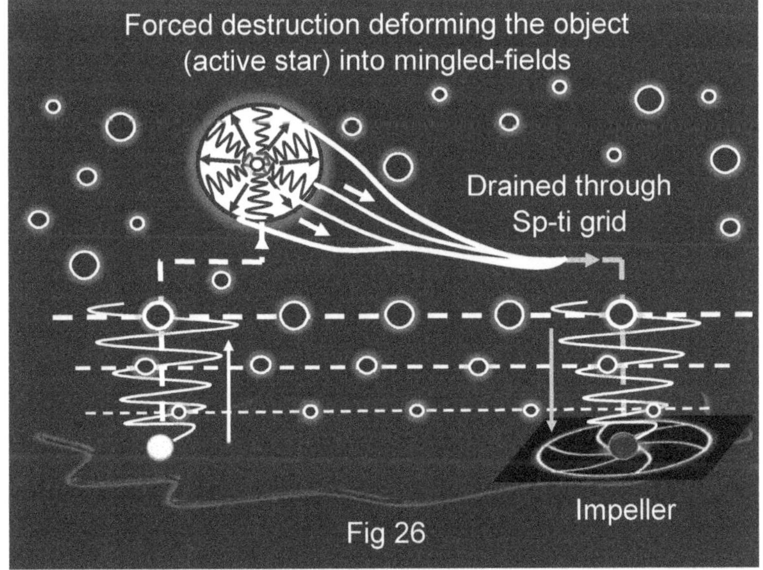

Fig 26

For creation on the other hand, the fundamental fields which are represented horizontally along with the sp-ti waves, due to the grid formation climbs up vertically like creepers. This helps in further evolution of fundamental particles in minute dimension, the objects yet floating in waves. Then the object grows along deep dimension to become a macro-scope object in wide dimension.

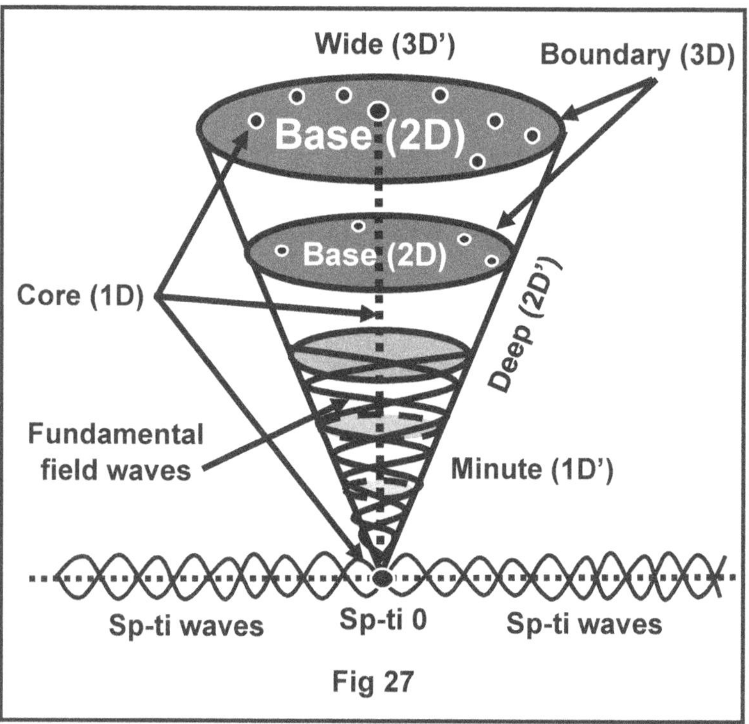

Fig 27

iv) Black holes - A deceptive appearance:

We will logically demonstrate to understand how there is no hole in the existence and it is only the absolute vacuum that appears as a hollow region. As we said earlier, even this hollowness is only pertaining to the medium and not object oriented. The region of space-time where the destruction process happens is initially a self-breakdown of an object such as a neutron star. As the object is spherical earlier, even after its breakdown we assume the hollowness created i.e., the black hole is also a spherical one. However, this darkness as a layer, is deeper than the spacious vacuum. Means, it is impossible to reach an inactive black hole. The spacious vacuum covers the black hole such that is would be confusing whether the black hole is away from us in terms of distance or depth. FTS has a key application to say the galaxy we live is actually a sphere that has a disc-like appearance with a black hole at its center when viewed from far away distance. This idea is opposite to that of Earth appearing flat when we are on it but actually a sphere when looked from space. The following illustration merely demonstrates a black hole that switches its appearance due to surface and depth difference, playing hide and seek with the observer, when he tries to reach to it. Means it is a well-like depth however, one can never fall into it.

1) For an idle black hole, observer will keep on trying to reach near to it, but faces one of the following two cases, i) The shadow relocates either by shifting forward or remaining deeper. ii) Disappears in half-way and gets re-centered even to the point where the observer started his journey itself.

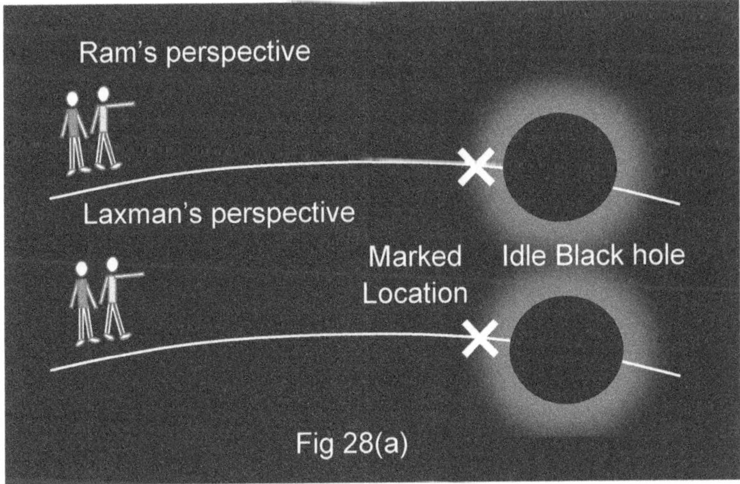

Fig 28(a)

2) Let us consider two observers Ram and Laxman watching an inactive black hole through a telescope. Ram decides to reach the

black hole and on reaching there, Laxman would still see his brother Ram and wave his hand.

3) Laxman finds no changes with Ram as he moves towards the black hole. However, Ram would see the appearance of black hole growing in size bigger and bigger and after certain point he would not see the black hole at all.

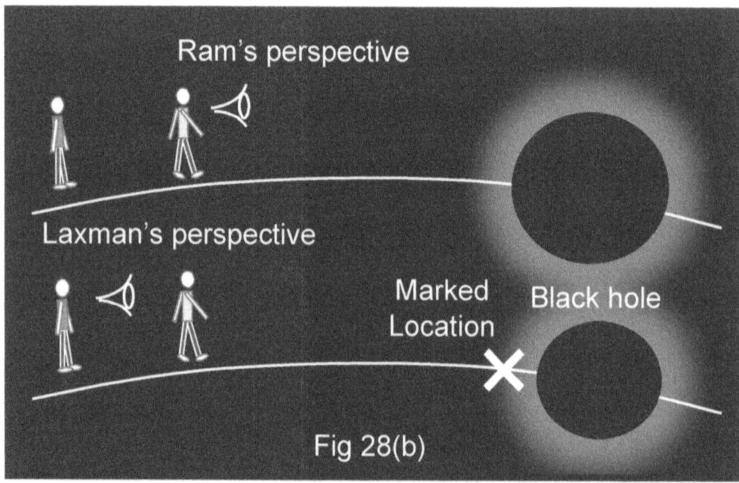

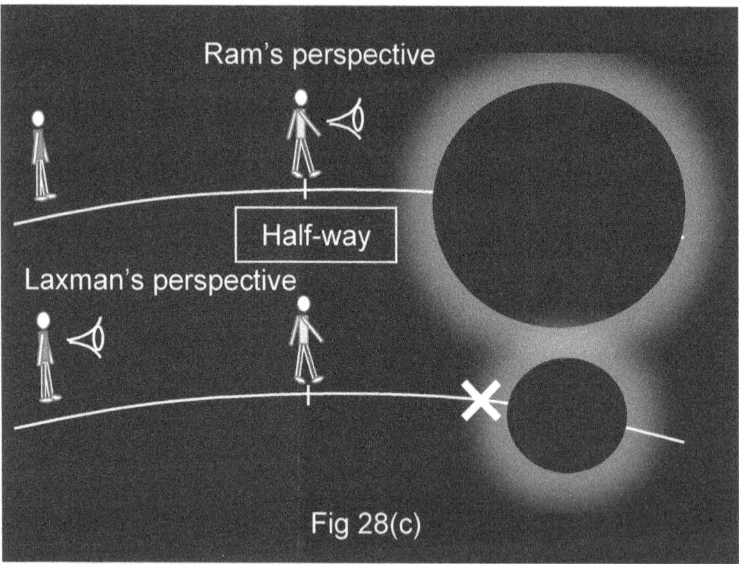

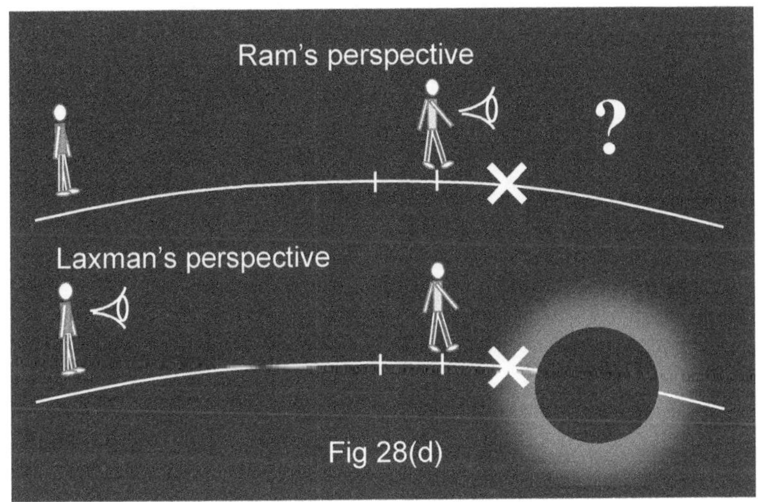

4) But Laxman still sees Ram as well as the destination of black hole to be reached, to be the same. Now, Ram reaches the destination and stops but sees no black hole there, looks back and get surprised by seeing the black hole near to Laxman.

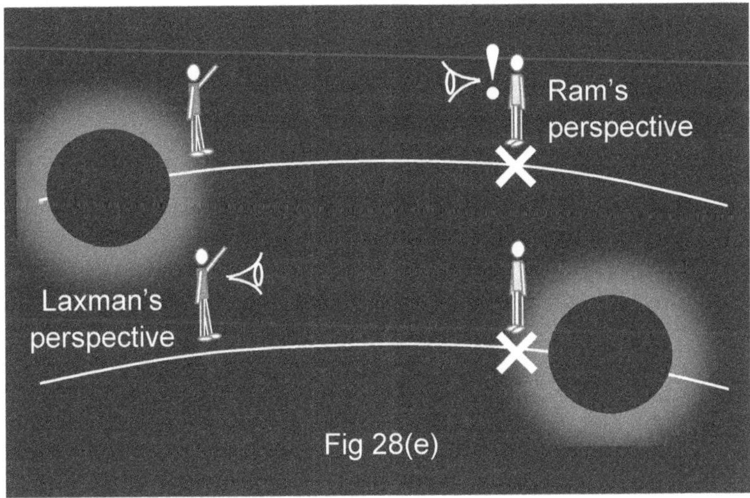

5) Laxman unaware of this, happily shows his hand to Ram for having successfully reached the destination and saying that he

could see him standing next to the black hole, which is another surprise for Ram.

6) Laxman now asks his brother Ram to further move into the event horizon of the black hole. Ram steps forwards and Laxman could no longer see him.

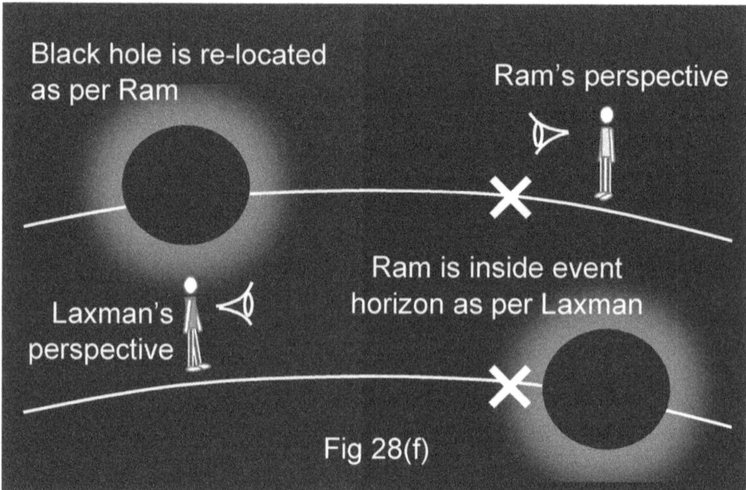

7) Ram could not see Laxman either and finds him to have entered into event horizon too. This is the duality concept of black hole for its appearance in 3D.

From the above idea, we shall understand that the black hole is situated at the core depth of the galaxy rather than a center of the disc appearance. It is the shadow of the entire galaxy, accumulated and seen as a center point on the surface level. Now, we shall also see the nature of active black holes and how this is not a hole but a deceptive appearance for human perspective, as follows.

We have already discussed in the nature of Sp-ti medium that the absolute vacuum and the Sp-ti liquid medium are dimensionally hidden nature and only the spacious vacuum is visible to us. Even the region where the destruction process happens is a flat space-time. At this region the impellers of destructive faces segregate, however, as usual the spacious vacuum configured with the Sp-ti grids remains the same. The internal bending of the Sp-ti lines that constitutes for the solidity of the object is collapsed by the time wheel. Thus, the object more like a liquid becomes flat to flow in a direction below which the grid lines drain the floods smoothly towards the singularity.

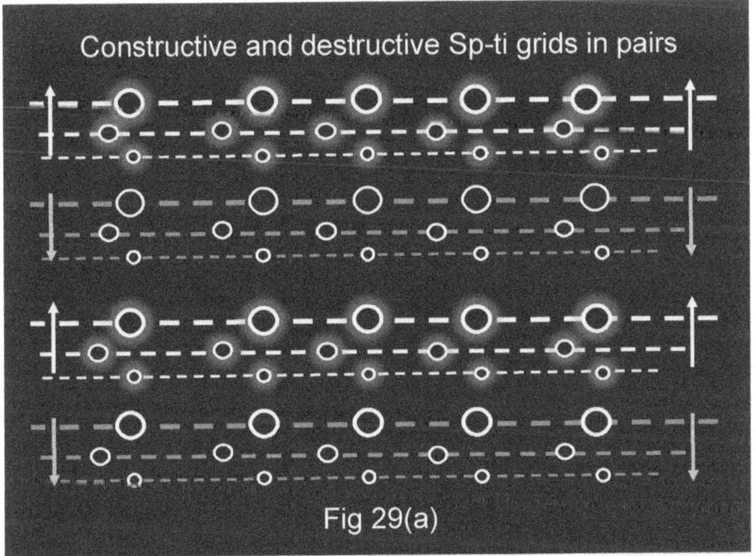

Fig 29(a)

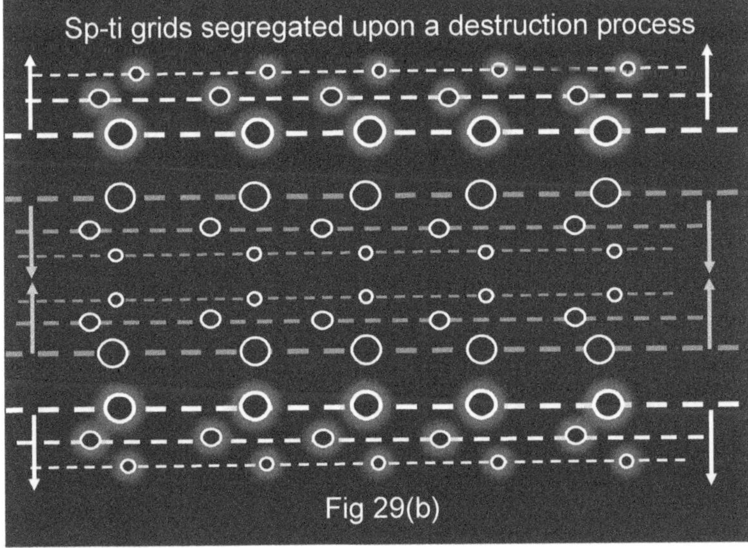

Fig 29(b)

Means, the grid lines are linear pertaining to the flat space-time. We shall imagine this segregation of destructive points to form a region around which the spacious medium for rest of the Universe still works, being away from it.

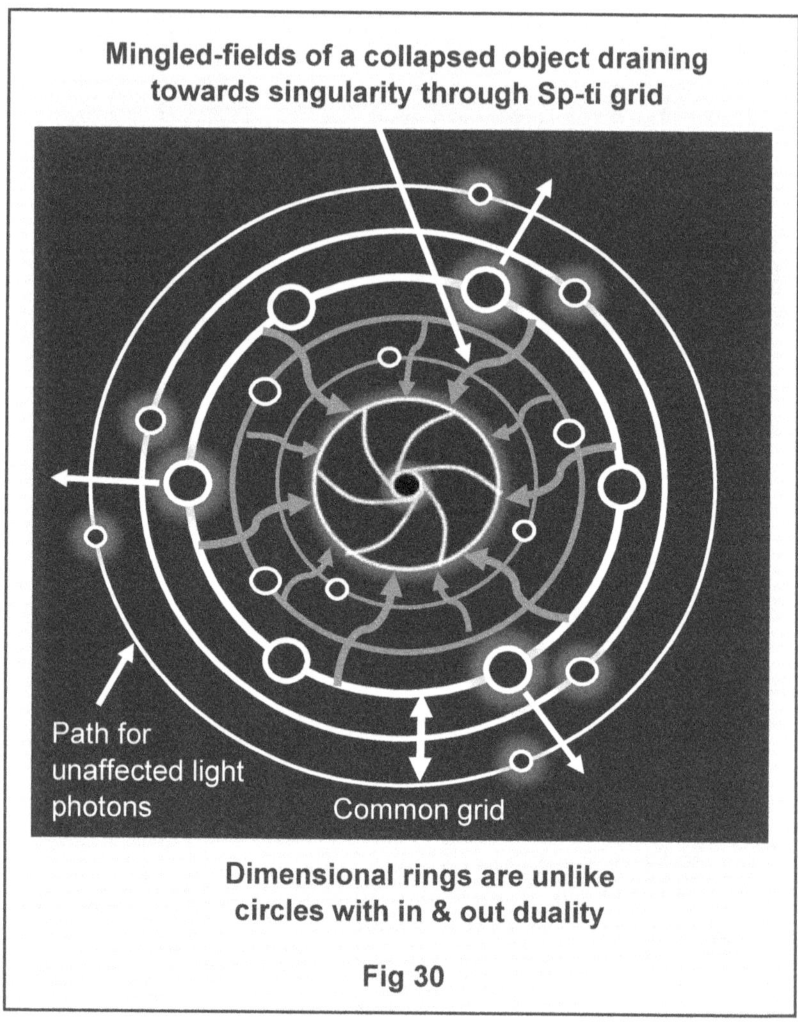

Dimensional rings are unlike circles with in & out duality

Fig 30

The dimensional rings are small and they grow in size depending upon the process, otherwise they are confined only to remain at the depth by being associated with core dimension. So, no black holes in existence, it is the absolute vacuum with an impeller, responsible for self-destruction of the object at its final time frame. It also forces the destruction by simply stirring the medium and collapse the solid nature of the nearby evolved objects. Then the mingled-fields flows towards the lower potential which is the Sp-ti 0 or singularity.

8.0 NEW THEORY OF GRAVITATION - INTRODUCTION

There are two ways to observe gravitation in real-time.

1) The river flows from mountain to the ocean. Where there is a difference in level between the two points and the water floods in the downward direction.

2) Now, the sea water turns into vapour by the sun's heat to form clouds, which is opposite to that of the previous case as the flow is from lower to upper level.

3) Then, the water vapour or the clouds precipitates to become heavy and pour down as rain, which is again from upper to lower level.

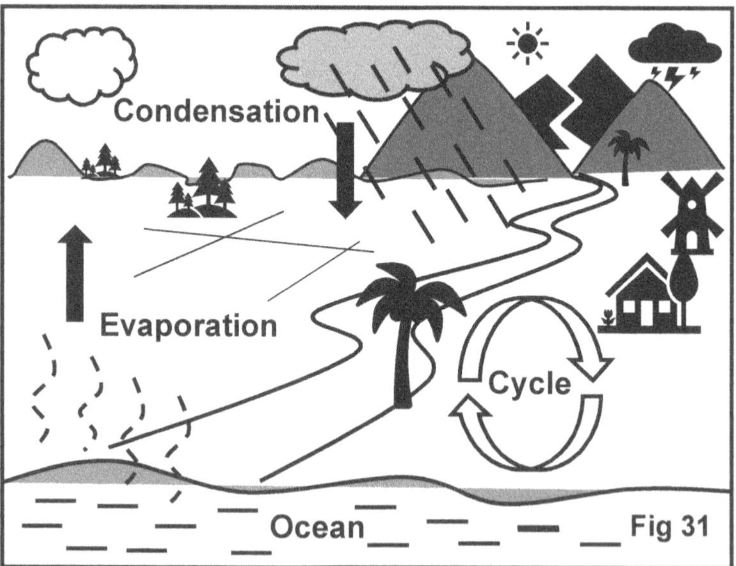

What are the basic ideas from the above understanding?

1) The level difference between two points is locally true to be Up and Down in terms of positions however, it is not about the direction of flow to be only in downward direction, as the process is bi-directional in a cycle.

2) The process involves two fluid mediums such as water and vapour which is same as liquid and gaseous medium, to be noted.

3) Now, when closely observed, heaviness and lightness are associated with the direction of flow, which conveys the meaning of gravitation, not to be a force but just a path to conduct the flow of certain process.

4) Heaviness is object oriented and causing a downward flow, whereas flow with the lightness is carried out in the opposite direction by the medium itself.

5) The packing of gas is an expanded form occupying more space and away from the accumulated or condensed nature of liquid form.

6) So, when the fluid medium is considered, liquid nature is closer to the point of Sp-ti 0 or singularity while the gaseous medium covers over the liquid which is obviously further away from the point of space zero.

7) Applying the above nature of fluidity with two mediums in space-time, gravitation is a bi-directional channel to conduct the flow of force or energy inward and outward.

8) Here, the outward flow means the external events happening in the Universe which is observable whereas the inward flow is the circulation of the very medium and about how the Universe is deeply rooted in space-time, which are dimensionally hidden for our noticing.

9) Heaviness as far as we know is about the solidity of the objects in terms of mass. The existing studies so far only knows that gravity is associated with mass however, gravity is independent of mass and mass required is only to demonstrate gravitation at macro-scale (General theory of relativity by Sir Albert Einstein).

We need to know the history and existing study of gravitation in brief to clearly differentiate the new study proposed in this book.

9.0 HISTORY AND EXISTING STUDY

The term Gravitation is popular since 1665, introduced by Sir Isaac Newton as he thought of what could be the reason behind an apple falling onto the ground straight downward from the tree. The earth must have an attracting force and that's why even the objects thrown upward from the earth are pulled back towards it, was the first level of understanding gravitation.

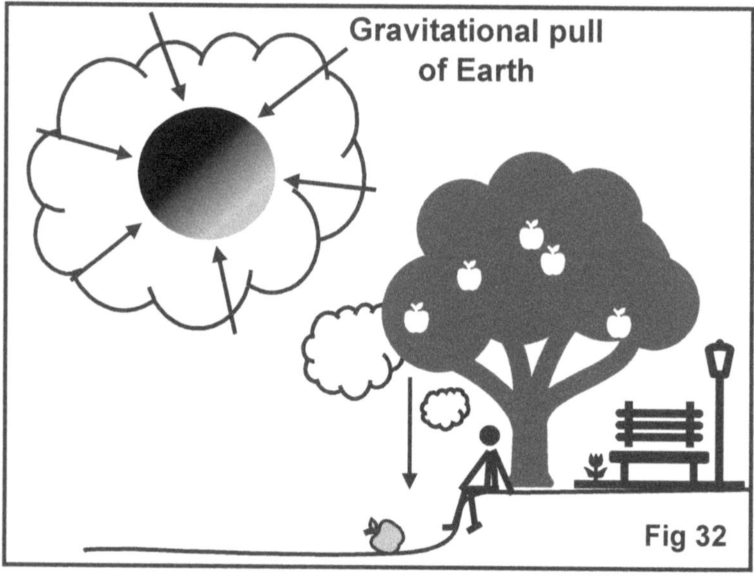

However, the moon beyond certain distance away from the earth is not falling into the earth but revolves around it, required a formula in common as follows,

$$F = G * \frac{m1 \times m2}{d^{\wedge}2}$$

F – Force of Gravitation

G – Gravitational constant

m – Mass of the object

d – Distance b/w the two objects

So, according to Newton, gravitational force involves two considered masses m1 and m2 and the distance 'd' between them. The formula of gravitation considered to be a force in all daily life calculations as well as in the prediction of planetary motions almost worked perfectly until the path of Mercury around the sun is observed closely. There is a precession in the orbit of mercury at the perihelion end. What could probably alter the path of the planet, shifting its major axis was not governed by the Newton's formula of gravitation. The planet revolving in free space has nothing to strain to change its path sharply and thus, the factor behind it was unknown. This mystery was unsolved over a couple of centuries.

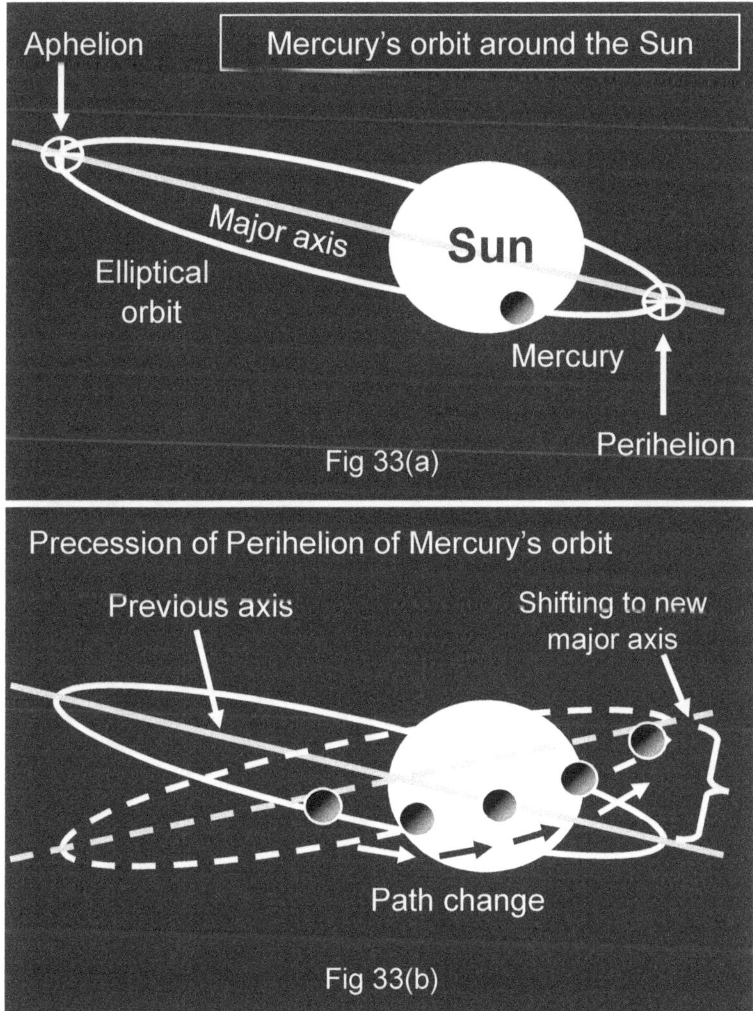

Fig 33(a)

Fig 33(b)

Later on, Sir Albert Einstein tried to find what is there in between Sun and the planet Mercury except the space. In his time period, he discovered the fact that space is not empty, open and free as we think but it behaves like a fabric for heavenly objects such as Sun, planets, moon and stars. Sir Albert Einstein actually discovered space-time to be a single-entity that together behaves like a fabric. If we assume space-time without objects is flat, then the heavenly objects cause curvature in it.

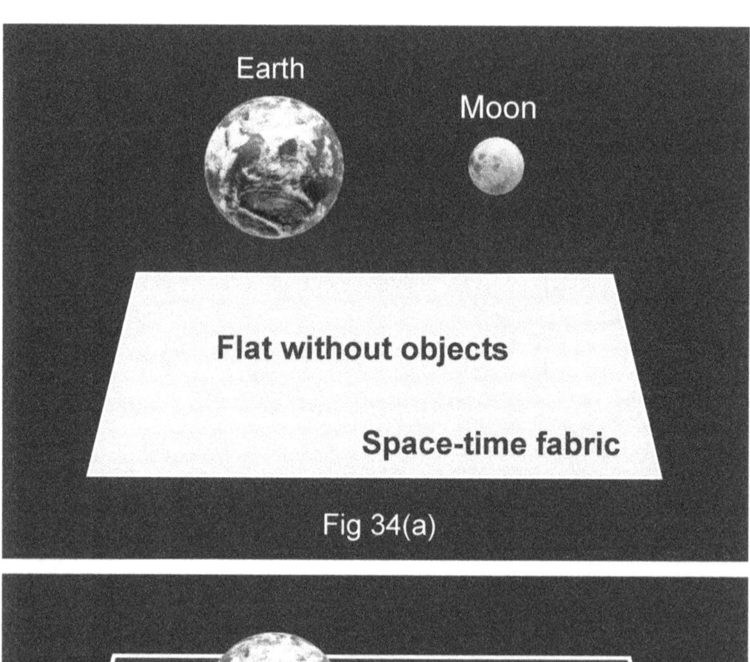

Fig 34(a)

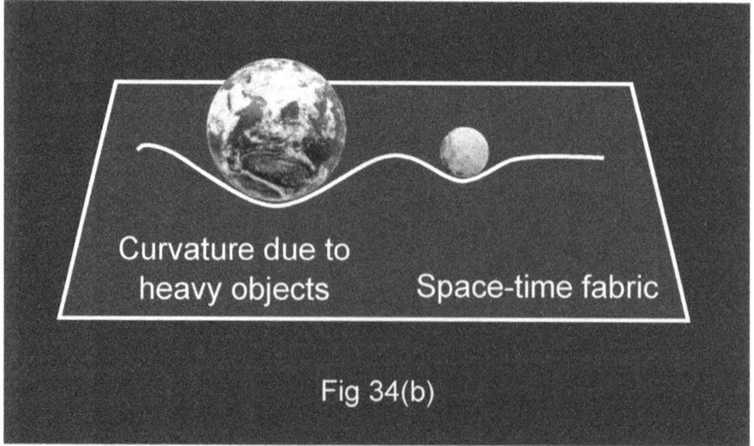

Fig 34(b)

The planet Mercury is subjected to some torque due to the motions of other planets along with this fabric in the solar system and thus had to change its path accordingly. This ground breaking discovery brought accuracy in the predictions of planetary motions more than Newton's formula of gravitation. Moreover, this precession was observed not only with Mercury but also with all the other planets revolving around the sun and the hidden factor is accounted in terms of curvature caused known as geometry of space-time. However, there is no up and down in space-time medium and it is a simple 2D representation for our understanding. Now, anyone would ask whether the curvature by the object is inward or outward and which one is right? There is a difference associated with the way it is curved that whether it is a pushing or pulling the space-time by the object.

The representation of single line drawn below the object with a curvature on the fabric shall be used to differentiate the depth of the curvatures between the two objects of different mass densities.

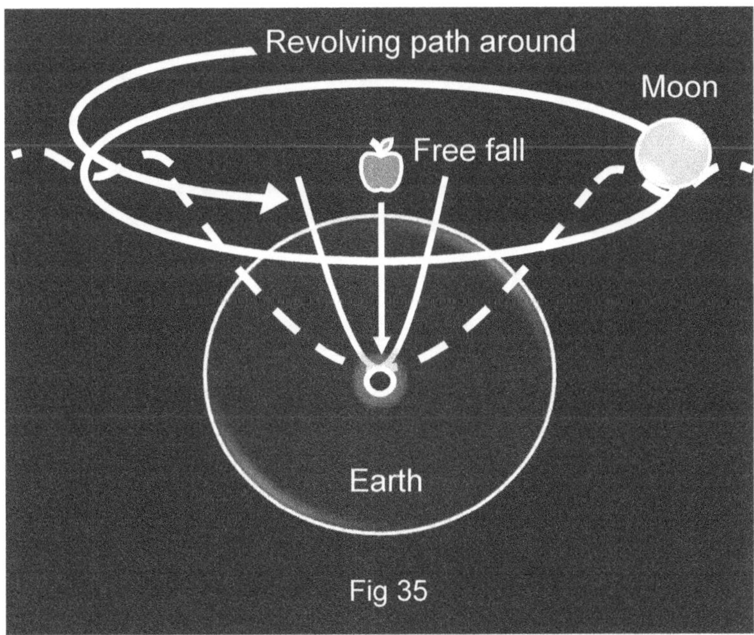

However, the curvature is actually from the surface of the object towards its core point which could cause a free space for an apple to fall into the Earth or a deeper curve for another object comparatively lesser heavy mass density such as the moon, located beyond certain limit that revolve around without falling into the Earth, as shown in Fig 35. Further, the curvature of space-time medium is drawn or bent by the big object such as an Earth in all the directions towards its core such that at any point all around the Earth, if the object is thrown up would come back to fall on the ground, is our general understanding.

10.0 THEORY OF RELATIVITY – TO BE SOLVED FOR ITS DUALITY

Sir Einstein derived a field equation, in which the matter & energy is equal to the geometry of curvature caused in space-time.

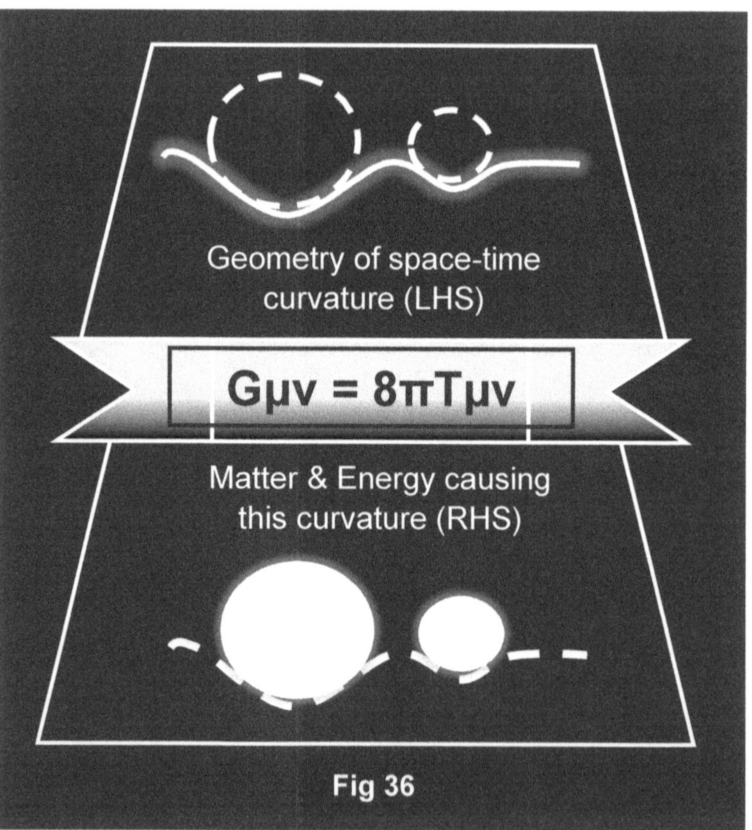

Fig 36

This is unlike Newton's formula which required factors such as two masses and a distance between them. Einstein tried to demonstrate gravitation to be like cause & effect rather than a force. The apple falling onto the ground or the moon revolving around the Earth are just the effects whose cause is nothing but the curvature in the medium. So, Einstein's gravitation model required at least one mass to cause the curvature in space- time.

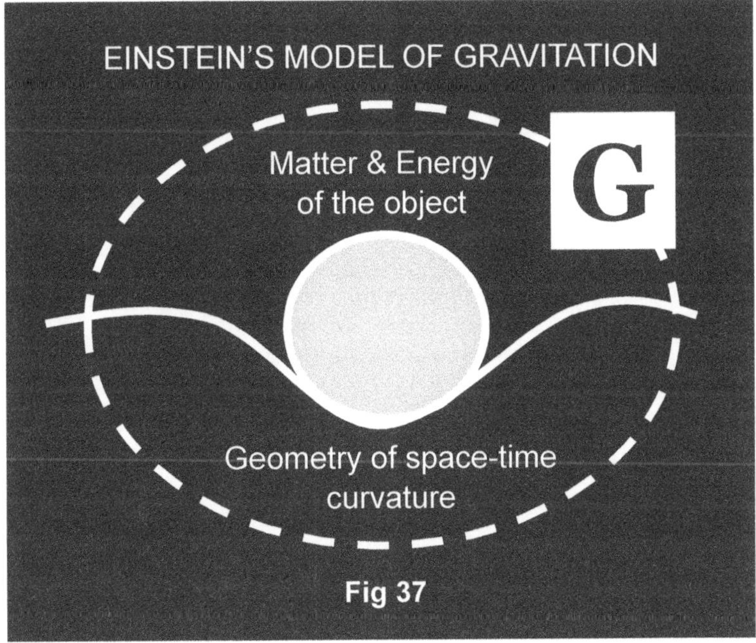

This gravitation model at macro-scale is not applicable for quantum physics. There is no such a setup of one object causing a curvature in the medium, enabling a nearby object to experience a gravity, at quantum scale. Thus, the scientists are unsatisfied and are trying to interpret something called quantum gravity in modern physics.

To solve the incompatibility between general theory of relativity (explaining gravitation only at macro-scale) and quantum mechanics (where the nature of gravity is unknown) in existing studies, is the main content of this book. The drawings and explanations of "New theory of gravitation" are based on the book "Fundamental Theory of Singularity (FTS)" published in the year 2024.

The major unknown fact about theory of relativity is, it is based on dual perspective or duality. Let us see the previous figures and analyze them once again. The field equation involves the matter & energy (LHS) as an accumulation which is more or less like a singular object and the curvature (RHS) caused by it, in the sp-ti medium. However, to physically observe the gravity, it requires a secondary dependent object such as an apple or a moon. Means, Sir Einstein managed to derive an equation that contains only the cause for gravitation and the effect is not considered. Cause & Effect is an inseparable duality and one of the examples is height & depth. It is impossible to separate this duality as it means in dual way that it is deeply high and highly deep as well. Now, even in the cause for gravitation we could see a duality that, the curvature in space-time is caused only as long as the object (matter & energy) exists. If no object then no curvature and in simple terms, **"matter tells space how to curve and space tells matter how to move"**. When a duality is equated on both the sides of the equation, it will get locked so perfectly and there is no way to derive a further step mathematically. Here comes the singular perspective to solve the major problems and mysteries in theoretical physics.

11.0 SPACE-TIME FABRIC AND ITS REAL NATURE

We shall pick up some important notes about Sp-ti fabric as described by Sir Albert Einstein available in existing studies.

1) Only the heavenly objects such as moon, planets, sun and stars are said to bend this fabric, means obviously there must be an object of certain heavy mass density that simply touches the fabric without causing a curvature in it.

2) A fabric is usually weaved with threads across length and breadth. If only the heavy objects are capable of bending this space-time fabric, then we should think of the thickness of the threads to be like a heavy rope network.

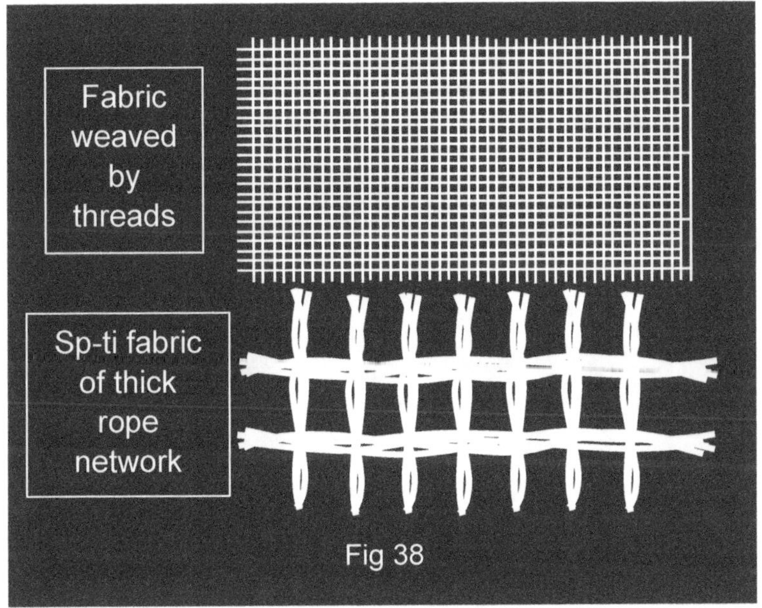

Fig 38

3) Now, we shall consider the above said object of certain heavy mass density that does not bend this heavy rope of certain thickness as reference object along with its reference lines for our further analysis of Sp-ti fabric.

4) Let this rope network be like a grid of space and time lines perpendicular to each other, holding this reference object as shown in Fig 39(a).

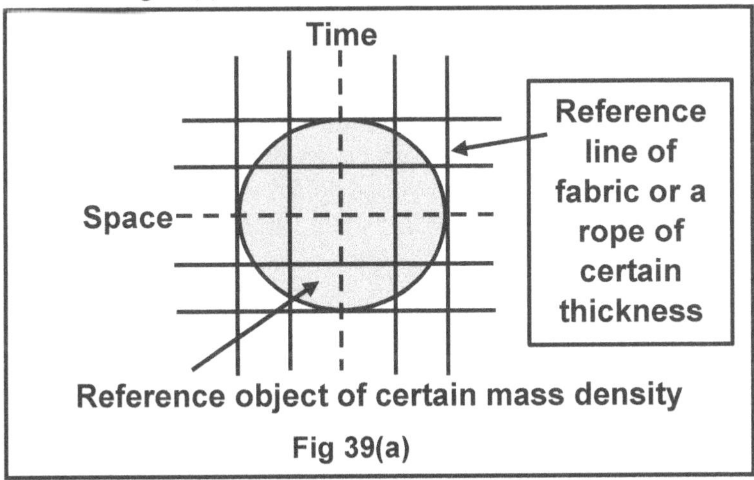

Fig 39(a)

5) This reference object with its sp-ti grid could be projected on its either side. If the objects of other mass densities like increasing heavy masses on LHS and decreasing less mass density objects on RHS are also associated with their corresponding Sp-ti grids or not?

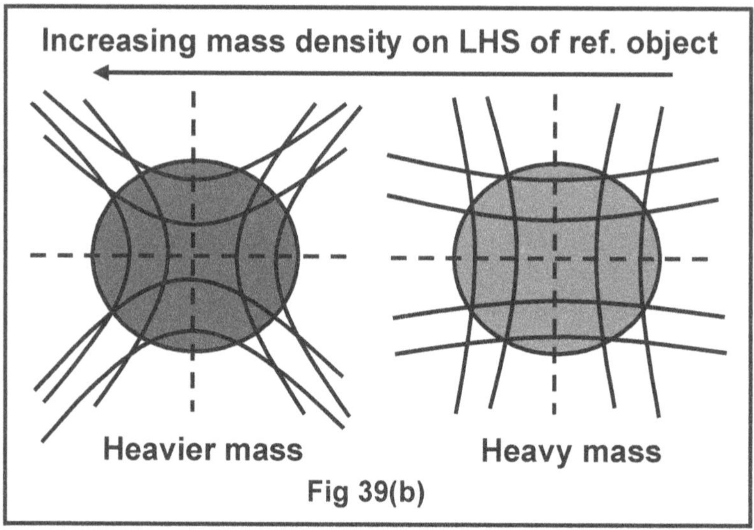

Fig 39(b)

6) As per Einstein's representation of heavy objects and the curvatures caused by them shows that the elastic nature of the medium does not vary from point to point but the depth of curvatures by the heavy objects differs among one another. Means, thickness of the rope of the Sp-ti fabric remains the same even for all the heavier objects more the reference object.

7) Now, what about the other side, whether the lesser mass density objects than the reference object have Sp-ti grid or not? The associated or corresponding Sp-ti grid lines of the object neither allows the small objects such as an apple to free fall nor the moon to revolve around with respect to the curvature caused in the fabric by the heavy object like Earth. So, even on the lesser density side (RHS), the Sp-ti grid must be absent obviously.

8) Unlike heavy masses, lighter masses could be graphed with same number of space-time lines however with thinner lines to

show the difference for the less mass densities in descending order. For our simple understanding, let the reference object be the Earth then the moon and the apple in the order of lesser mass density objects along with their grids in space-time are as shown in Fig 40.

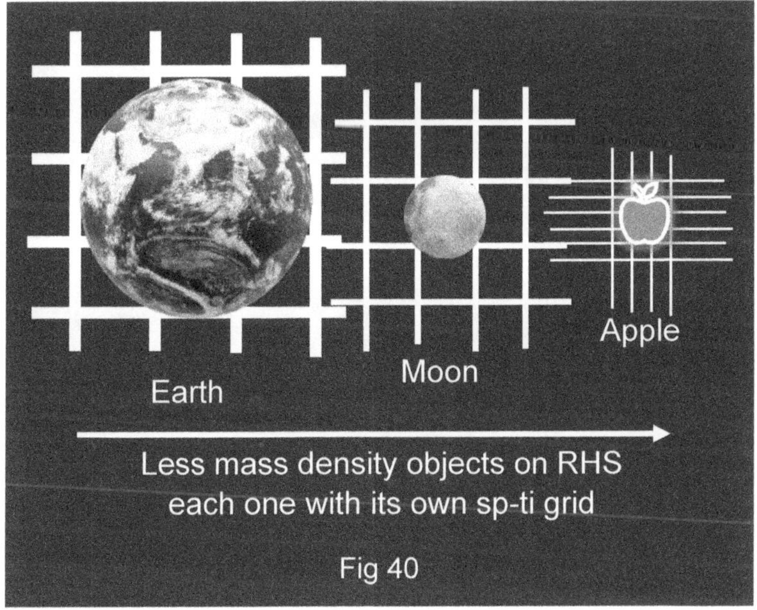

Fig 40

9) Now in this way, even if the heavy mass object causes a curvature in sp-ti fabric, the smaller or lighter objects does not have a dependency factor for gravitation. So, when we could think of how gravitation works, it is possible to know the condition in which gravitation absolutely does not work too.

10) However, the above ideas need technical background to bring out all the hidden details unknown in existing studies. As the limits of space-time fabric are unknown in theory of relativity, the representation is wrongly extended as shown in Fig 41, where the curvature of sun is more than the Earth and next to the sun, the curve caused by the black hole is shown to be steep and the end point is unknown, called as Singularity (point of no return).

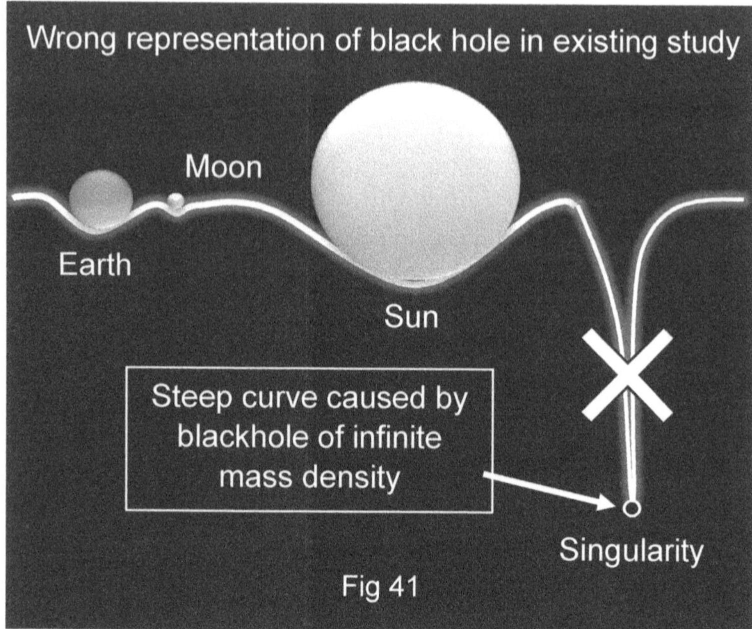

Fig 41

11) Our new study starts from here, to go deeper with singular perspective based on Fundamental Theory of Singularity (FTS). We will track all the objects of the Universe in terms of their mass densities and plotted in the Sp-ti grid that serves as a graph. In that way, we would know how the Sp-ti grid is supposed to be at the background and probably what are all the changes happened thereby.

12) The quantum scale must have emerged from a point which is a black hole. On the other hand, macro-scale objects such as a neutron star breaks down to form a black hole. So, the space-time configuration itself begins from a point and ends in a point, meaning space-time is finite. We will see a clear and complete explanation for the same.

12.0 NON-WORKING CONDITION OF GRAVITATION

Sir Isaac Newton followed by Sir Albert Einstein and the physicists of the world thought of how gravitation works. And the existing understanding is, gravitation is happening due to the curvature caused by the heavy objects in space-time fabric. If it is questioned what could be the condition for gravitation that does not work, anybody would say if the heavy objects do not bend the fabric or the space-time itself does not behave like a fabric, then no gravitation at macro-scale.

However, it is like coming up with an idea and if asked for further details then stepping back to the previous level. The answer is, the dependency factor for gravitation is common between the two considered objects. Of which, one object could be defined as, ability of the object to cause a curvature that extends a dependency and the other one to have the inability to fall for this dependency. Which means, even if a heavy object like Earth causes a curvature, the apple or the moon with its own Sp-ti grid does not undergo a gravitational effect. Only the absence of corresponding grid could cause the inability for these secondary dependent objects, to be noted.

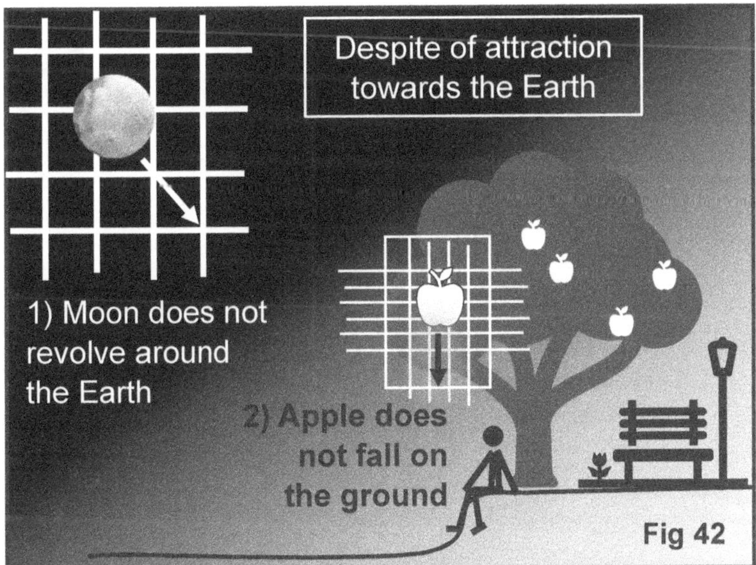

Now the question is, then what is the significance of curvature caused in the medium that does not have any effects? Answer is, the curvature still has an effect that the objects are just stopped by their grid but still has an attraction towards the deeper point which is same like the river water stopped by the dam, still has its pressure against the wall trying to flow towards the lower potential.

13.0 FURTHER ANALYSIS OF SPACE-TIME FABRIC

Technically speaking, the non-working condition of gravitation is different from no gravitation at all. Fig 42 shows, despite of the curvature caused by Earth in Sp-ti medium, the effects such as falling of an apple towards the ground and revolution of moon around the Earth are not happening. Here, the gravitation is actually present and only the working mechanism is held.

We will study the Sp-ti grid configuration in detail. Space-time to be like a fabric is acceptable as long as its limitations are not met. Fabric has the elastic nature and at which point it will breakdown is not explained or analyzed in general theory of relativity. Even though the black holes were predicted through calculations, the space-time is said to be warped and also gravity is said to be high inside a blackhole. These two are misconceptions in existing studies and clarification for the same shall be discussed in fore coming topics. As discussed in the introduction part, we are going to apply the fluidity rather than an elasticity to describe the nature of space-time medium.

Technical analysis starts with choosing the ideal object for drawings and representations which must be a sphere, a circle in 2D. Now, we consider the reference object along with its reference grid as shown in Fig 39(a), which is a general representation. The object appears to have no connection with the grid. We all know the object must have evolved in the medium, in that case the representation has the following changes,

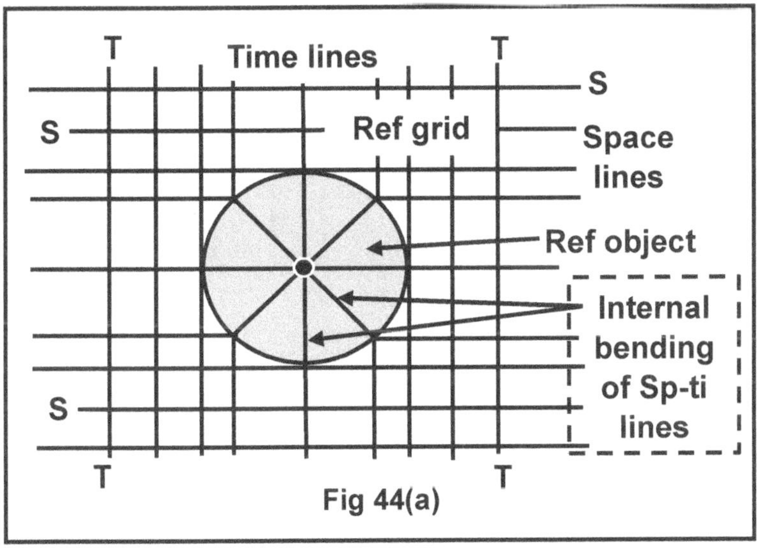

Fig 44(a)

There is an internal bending of sp-ti lines by the volume of the object. However, this bending of space-time is the first and foremost one, not described in theory of relativity. Let us forget about the object to have evolved with combination of atoms and elements in the universe but just assume, it has grown like a fruit. Fig 44(a) shows, the object has a tight packing in the Sp-ti grid. Simply for growth and mobility of an object, there must be a free space to permit the same. How come the medium provides such a space, is nothing but the compensation in terms of elastic property.

Let us project this unused space or space-time available for the object with the following modifications.

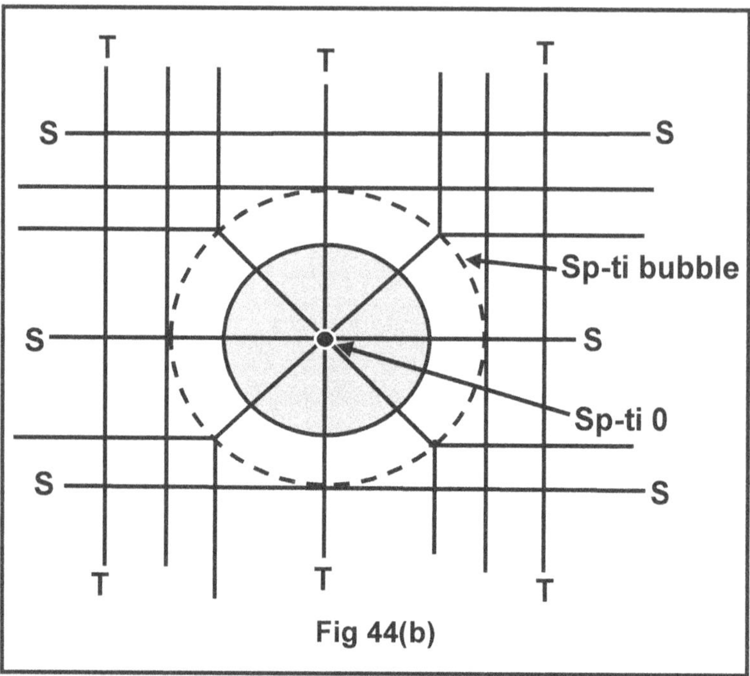

Fig 44(b)

Fig 44(b) is the technical representation of singular object in Sp-ti medium. Where the sp-ti bubble is the special aspect to show the available space-time of an object and Sp-ti 0 is the point indicating no space no time for an object, means only the Sp-ti medium exists at that point. From here, it is possible to formulate the technical study of space-time. Now, we will discuss on the most complicated problem that prevents anyone to access the knowledge of space-time. It is the size factor. Size usually denotes the volume of the object. This would impose a confusion between large object with less mass density and small object with heavy mass density which is impossible to plot the objects of the Universe in the sp-ti grid in a row that starts from the point of Sp-ti 0. It sounds like a simple issue and could be resolved but there is no way to sort it out straight away. Diplomatic way of approach is required.

Clearly, as only the heavy mass density objects could bend the sp-ti lines (rope network) we marked a reference object of certain heavy mass density to be minimum point that the object simply touches the fabric without causing a curve. We need a simple experimentation setup to bring out some more details as follows.

An embroidery hoop set with a fabric could be felt for its elasticity with some tension. Now, a single object of certain mass density that does not bend and curve the fabric is assumed to be kept on it. When we press this object against the fabric, for sure the curvature is caused and could be visibly seen right underside of the fabric setup.

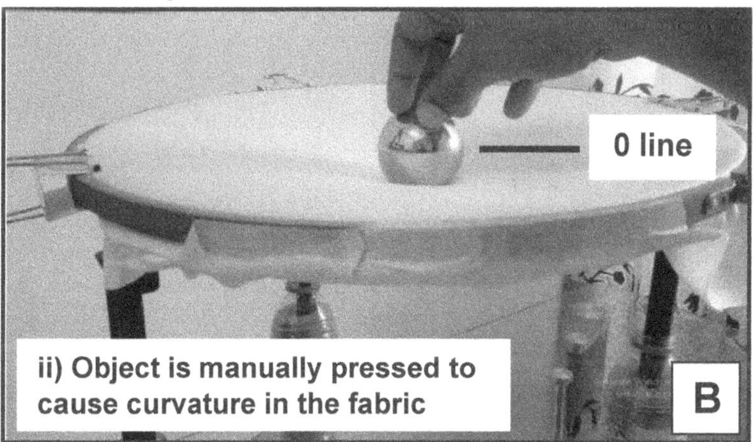

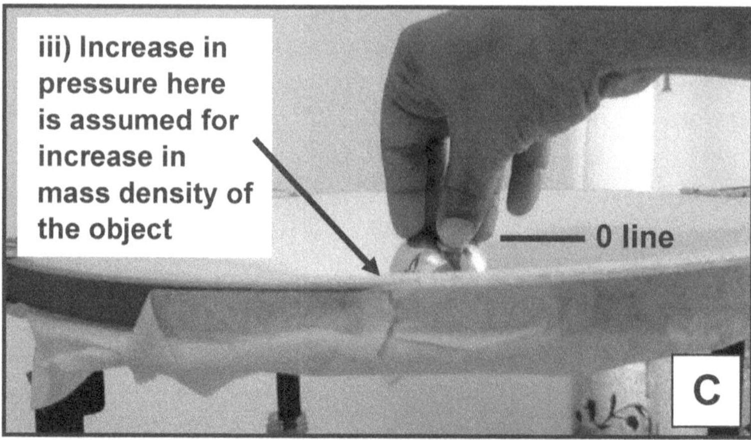

This pressure applied to the object shall be considered for increase in mass density of the object. It enables us to mark three points from the reference point of zero curve in the fabric towards a curvature of high mass density (3) gone through low (1) and medium (2) mass density points.

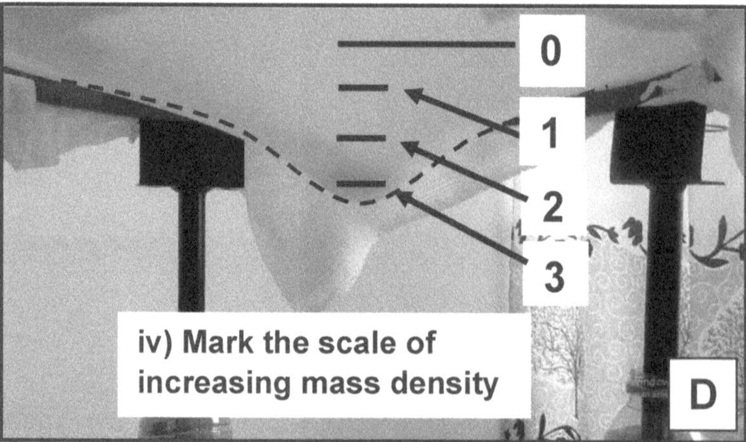

Now, next to the reference ball that is lying on the fabric, we keep another ball whose mass density is lesser than the reference ball. This ball also obviously does not curve the fabric however, what difference it makes compared to the reference ball?

In real-time this ball comes to the position of -1 above ref. object which is at zero. Further decrease in mass density occupies -2, -3 and so on in a scale.

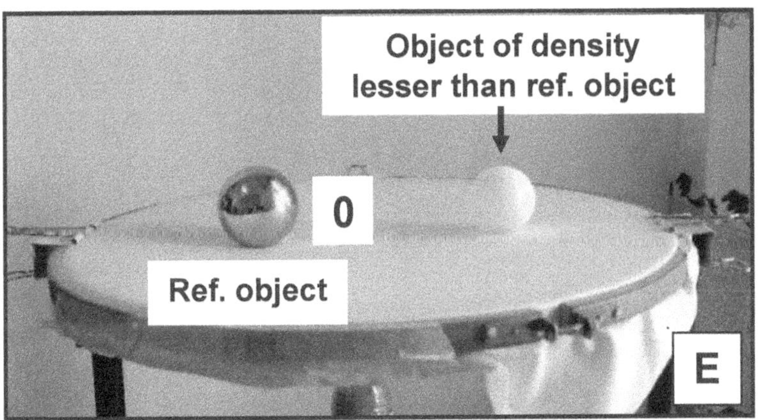

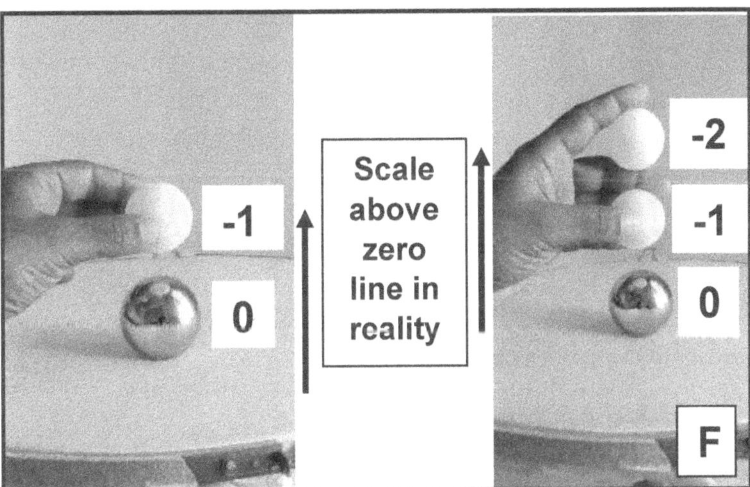

Having said that we are going to apply singular perspective based on FTS, is it required two or more objects to analyze different mass densities in space-time? No. The above experimentation with many objects is just for visualization. When it comes to the representation it would be a single object henceforth.

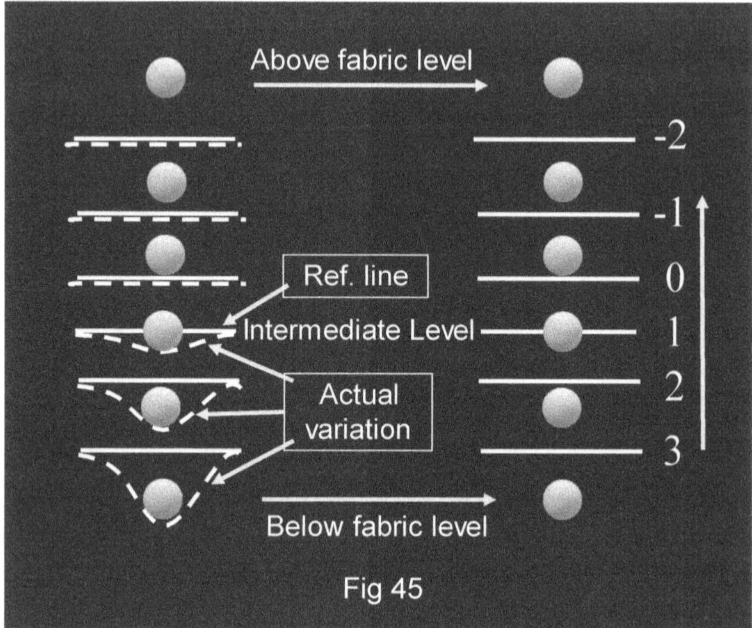

Fig 45

Fig 45 has a representation that captures some of the details about Sp-ti fabric. Here, the reference line remains unchanged and the dotted lines shows the actual variation i.e., the curvature caused by the heavy object. We observe that, as the mass density of the object decreases, it is moving away from the fabric. We can trace the object from below the reference line of fabric to cross the intermediate level for some density value and then detach to reach the point above fabric level. The variation is marked through the values +3, 2, 1, 0, -1 -2.

Now, how to represent objects of various mass densities towards or away from the reference line of Sp-ti fabric, without any values and even the dotted lines indicating the actual variation.

And as said earlier, we are going to use only a single object to show the variations such that the object of certain mass density would simply touch this ref line or rope and the objects of less mass densities would be away from this rope as well. How is it possible?

For this, we make use of an idea in our daily life that, when an object is moving away from the observer, it appears smaller and smaller and completely vanishes from sight at certain point. Here, the object never undergoes any actual change in volume or mass and it is just an appearance. So, when we use a singular object for the representations, it is possible to show the variation just only with the size factor such that when the mass density of the object decreases, the size of the object is reduced and could be shown away from the reference rope as well, same object at different positions as shown in Fig 46.

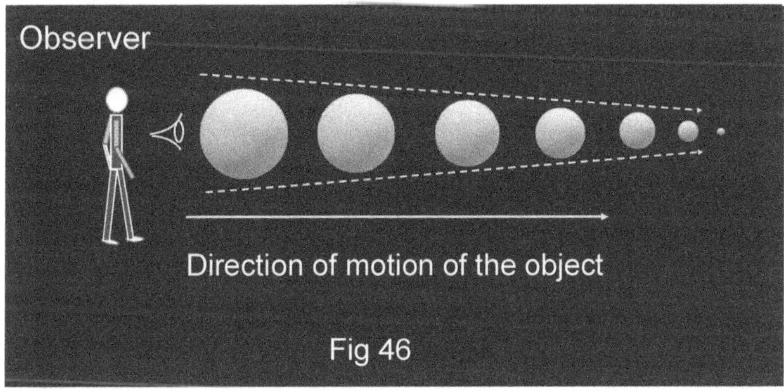

Fig 46

Note 1: Reducing size of the same object at different positions does not undergo actual variation in its mass or volume (Appearance only).

Note 2: Size factor shall be used to indicate various mass densities of the object only and it is not about the volume of the object in space-time study at all.

Here, if a reference line picked from the sp-ti fabric is marked at the initial position of the object near to the observer Fig 47 (Representation A) then the objects away from realizing this line or rope could be shown at different positions where the reduced size of the same object represents the less mass density object away from the reference object touching this line. Representation B is useful to plot the objects from macro to Nano scale till it reaches the point of zero mass density.

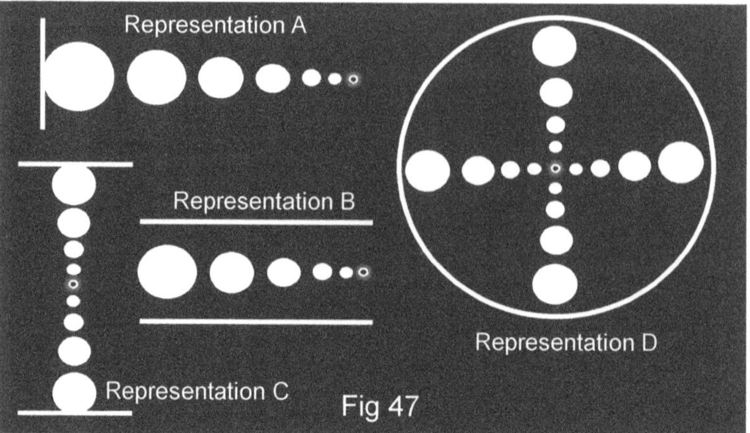

Zero mass point is also called as space-zero time zero or simply sp-ti 0 point. All the representations here do not indicate any distance, direction and even in & out duality of a circle to be noted. Now what about the objects of high mass densities beyond the rope?

If we continue to track in this way, then obviously there must be a point where an object of certain heavy mass would break this rope from bearing it. We move on with new ideas about space-time, which are obviously unavailable in existing studies. The general theory of relativity explains the medium of space-time to have fabric behavior and string theory on the other hand explains the first level objects i.e., the fundamental particles to behave like rubber bands or strings. The fabric bends or curves with any objects placed on it and becomes flat when removed, same way the rubber band could be stretched and if left, it restores. One thing common in both the cases, is the elastic nature. We call the Universe to be a cosmic ocean. What is the purpose of elasticity or elastic nature in an ocean? There is another nature with same property and more flexible than elasticity called as 'fluidity'.

Complication in space-time study:

1) We called the sp-ti fabric to be a thick rope network, as it is only the heavy objects that can bend it. However, we have to think it in real-time that, which one is greater, rope or the object? In our

daily life, we use the rope to tie the objects, means the object must be under the control of rope. If the rope is held loose for the tied object to move or slip out, then the rope loses its purpose. So, even in case of Sp-ti medium, the heavy objects cannot bend this rope. Then, do we mean this rope is used to tie the heavy objects of the Universe? The answer is yes, but how?

2) Further, we call the unbending rope as "Gravitational rope". If this rope being the reference line picked up from the Sp-ti fabric and it is not bending means, where did the elasticity vanish? and what does the curvature in the Einstein's representation (Fig 37) actually means? Here applies the fluid nature of space-time medium, shall be discussed in detail under the following topic Sp-ti grid configuration.

14.0 SPACE-TIME GRID CONFIGURATION AND FLUIDITY OF SP-TI MEDIUM

We build a Sp-ti grid configuration from the basic representation of an object with its own Sp-ti bubble meant for its growth and motion, Fig 44(b). For which we use Representation model B from Fig 47.

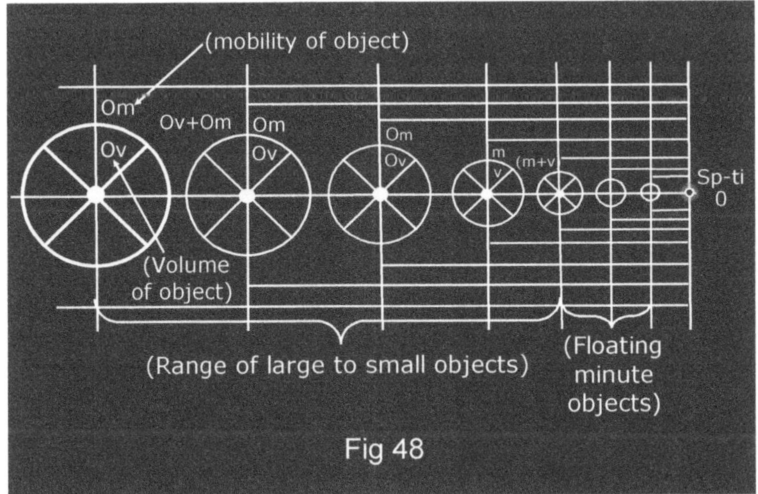

Fig 48

Fig 48 shows, there is a range of large to small objects that has internal bending of sp-ti lines and beyond which the objects such as atoms and particles could not bend the lines and are said to be floating or minute objects. The configuration reaches the starting or emerging point, which is a black hole or simply Sp-ti 0. The medium provides a permissible space for the volume **(Ov)** and mobility of the object **(Om)**. The shape of the Sp-ti bubble is unseen here, as the objects of various mass densities are plotted in a row till Sp-ti 0. However, it is possible to see the bubble by comparing two considered objects of different mass densities significantly at two different positions as shown (Fig 49).

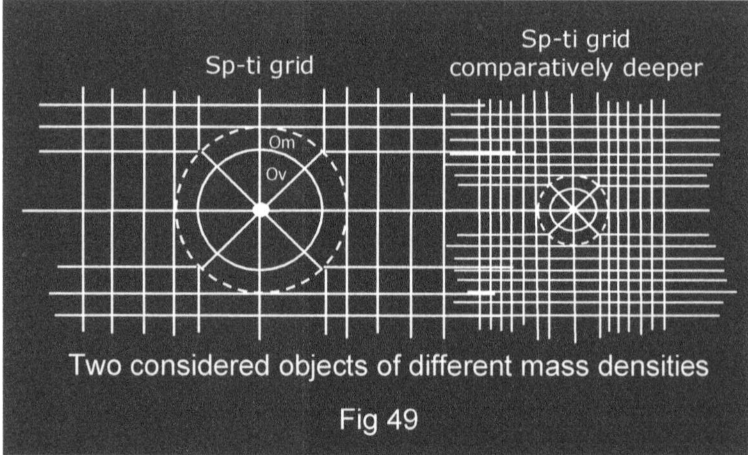

Fig 49

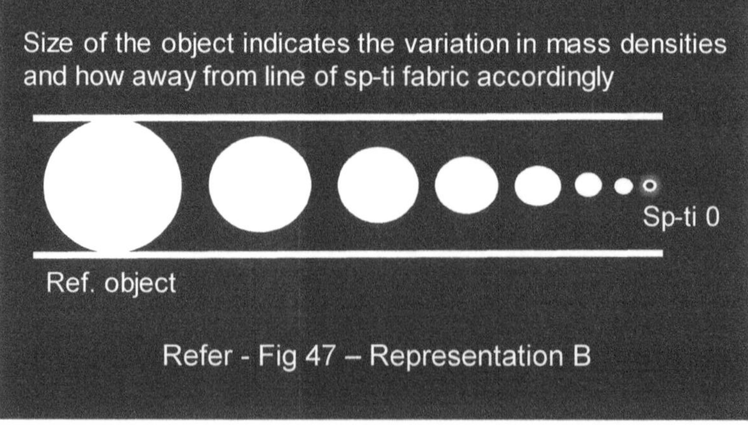

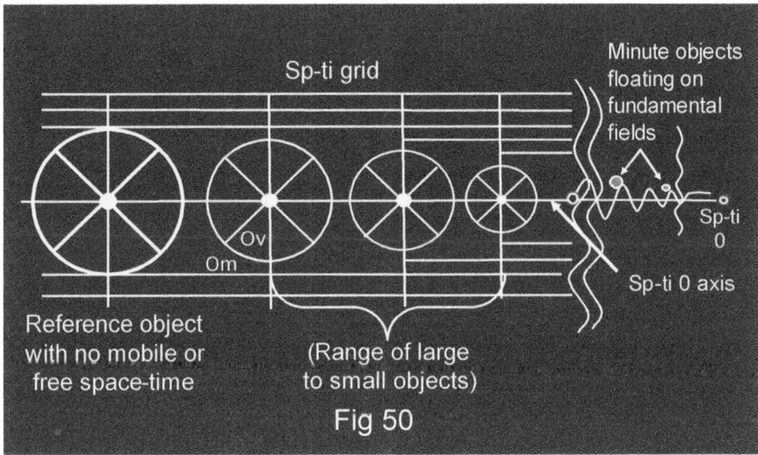

Fig 50

Fig 50 is a simplified Sp-ti grid where the reference object is also marked. We can observe that, there is no free space-time available for the reference object for its motion, as it has used it up with its heavy mass density. Means, the object has touched the reference line and has to roll on the fabric for its motion. Now, how to represent the objects heavier with increasing mass density than reference object? Tracking of which we would know what is actually a curvature in Sp-ti medium caused by the heavy objects.

We see all the objects in the grid have same number of internal sp-ti lines including the reference object. Now, for a further increase in mass density it is possible to increase the thickness of the Sp-ti lines to show the difference but we very well know that the Sp-ti fabric itself has certain unchanging thickness of a rope network and so the corresponding reference object marked on it. Secondly, we cannot increase the length of the Sp-ti lines further and show it a bigger object, as the reference object itself has already touched the line of fabric and the macro-scale is closed with parallel lines and finite in nature. Now, shall we go on for bending of external Sp-ti lines of the medium, as we already have seen in Fig 39(b)? No, before that we have some minute details to analyze.

Let us consider the volume and mass of the objects in terms of Sp-ti lines internally bent by the object. Even though the volume and mass of the object are more or less the same that, there is no volume without mass, it is still possible to compare the volume and mass of the object in terms of internal bending sp-ti lines.

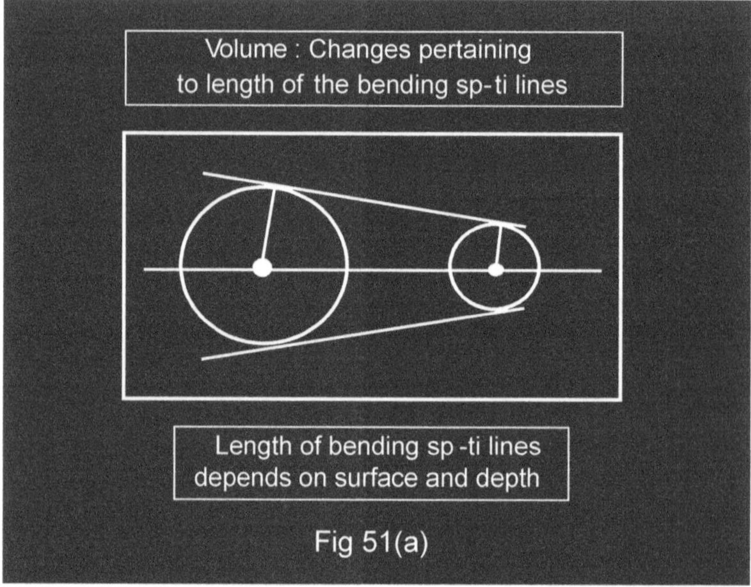

Fig 51(a)

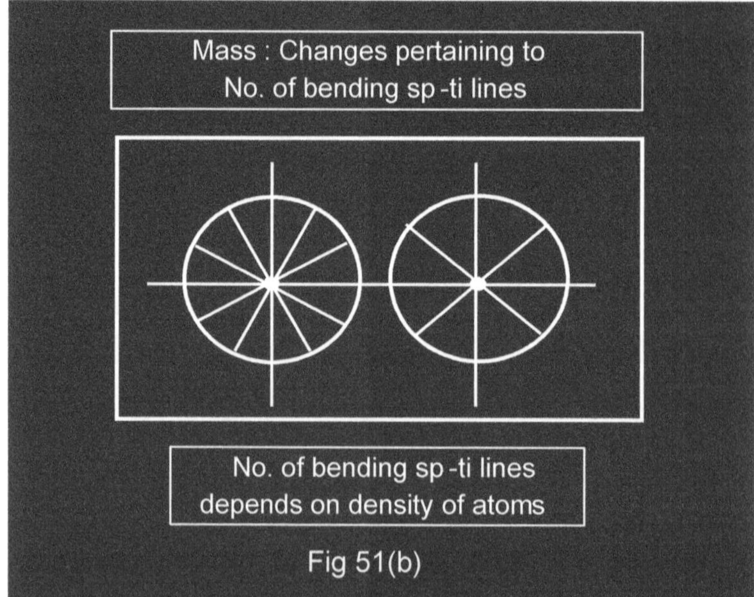

Fig 51(b)

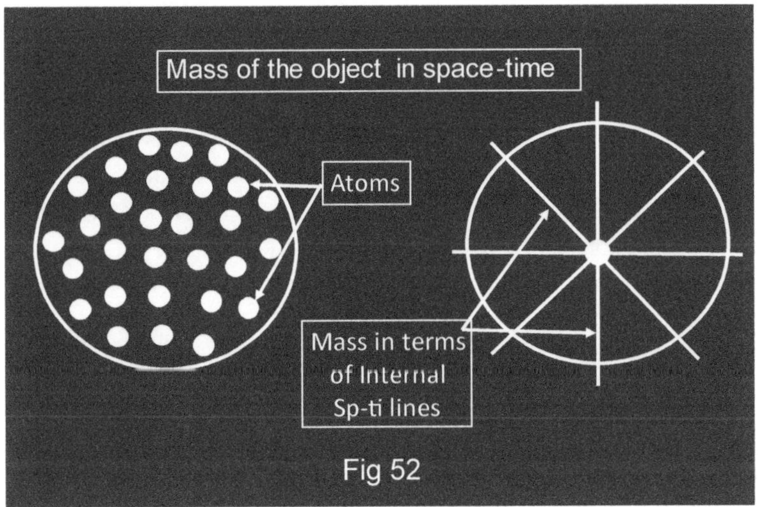

Now, with respect to the number of sp-ti lines, let the objects be differentiated as less, average and more mass densities as follows,

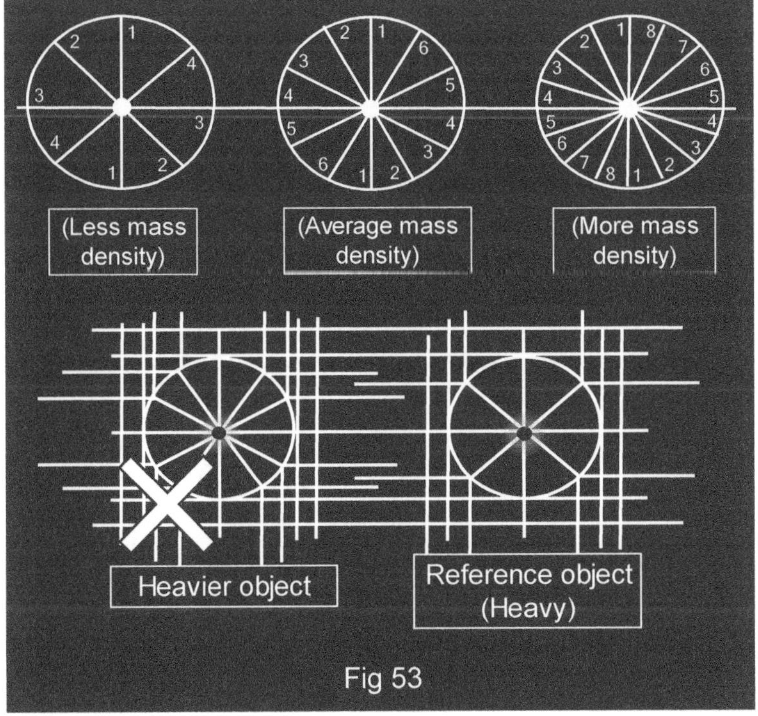

Ideally the number of internal Sp-ti lines must have a corresponding external sp-ti lines to connect. In that case, the Sp-ti medium remains infinite. Then, what could possibly connect to the increasing internal Sp-ti lines for increasing mass density of the objects beyond the reference object to compensate here? It is nothing but the nature of the medium. Elastic nature of the fabric is not encountered so far, as we have clarified that the rope as well as the Sp-ti grid lines does not bend for the objects. Thus, here applies the fluidity. The Sp-ti grid surrounding the object as shown in Fig 49 is due to the fluid nature of Sp-ti medium like the object in deep water is surrounded by the medium in all the directions.

The fluidity in space-time medium is invisible till its tolerance is touched by the reference object and thereby increasing mass density is utilizing the tolerance which is indicated with the curvature. This is same as the Einstein's representation of curvature in Sp-ti fabric but it is the tolerance of fluid medium indeed. Now, we will see some real-time examples to pick up the ideas to apply the fluid nature.

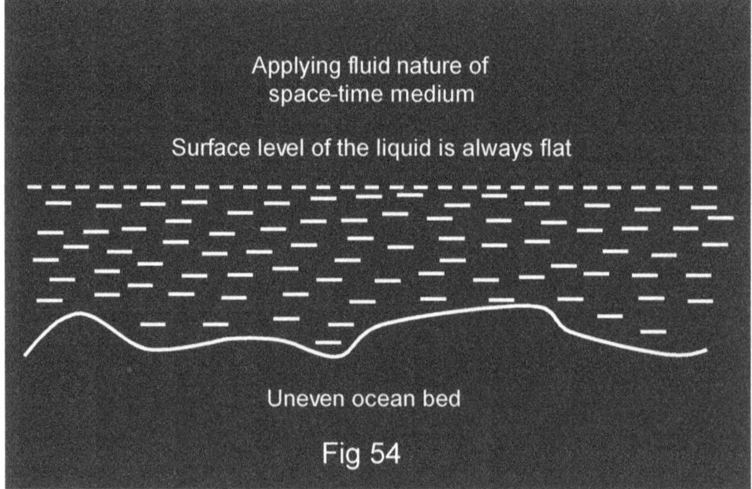

Fig 54

Let us assume that, an uneven land surface is filling with water. When the water level raises, the crests and troughs at its depth is not seen on its surface. Means, the surface of liquid is always flat.

According to fundamental theory of singularity, the space-time in liquid form is an ocean at the depth of the medium which is hidden dimensionally. The Universe we live is the only the surface of this sp-ti ocean. So, when we apply the fluid nature in 2D representation we get two surfaces above and below the heavy object. There is a curvature represented with dotted lines towards the axis as the mass density of the object increases.

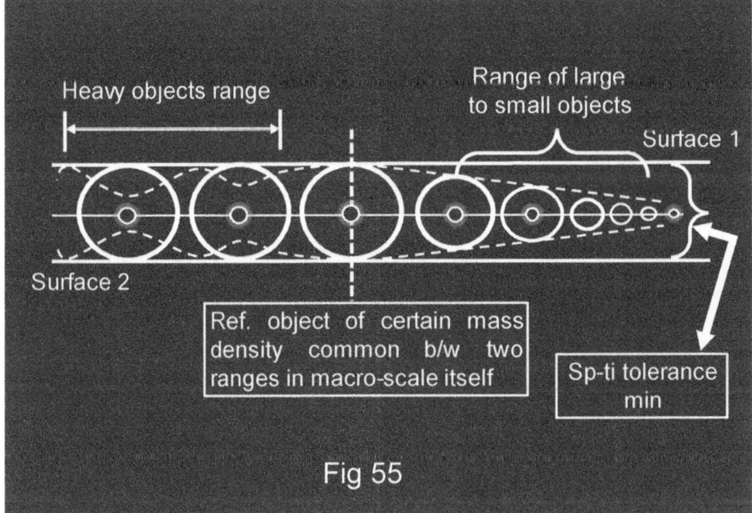

Fig 55 conveys some important notes about sp-ti medium

1) If all the objects of the Universe are arranged in row in terms of their mass density, the scale emerging from Sp-ti 0 need not be infinite. Surface of fluidity provides parallel lines to accommodate the heavy mass density objects within the two lines and the variations could be shown with increasing curve with respect to increasing mass density.

2) The reference object is the first heavy object to touch the tolerance limit of the fluid medium and this minimum point that does not cause a curvature is called as Sp-ti tolerance min. Now, it is obvious that, what is the maximum limit of this increasing curve. As the surfaces are accommodating the heavy object from above and below, the two symmetrical curves touch at the center,

which could be drawn as a line or axis called as Sp-ti tolerance max. What will happen if the tolerance curve by the heavy mass density object reaches the maximum limit is the next topic of discussion.

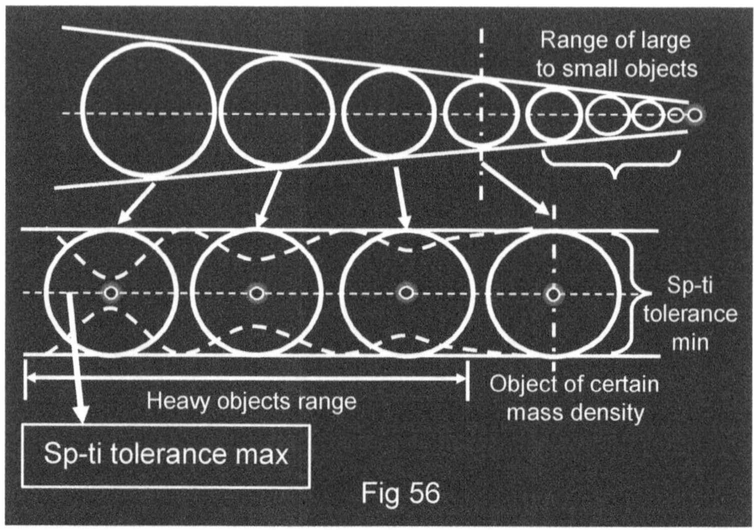

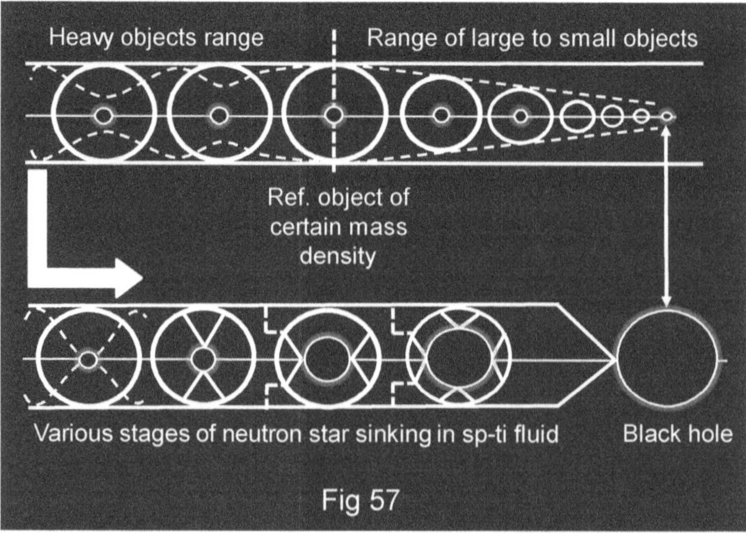

3) In the order of increasing mass density, we encounter a neutron star. The line marked for the maximum limit for such an object is

called as Chandrashekar limit. As we know, he is an Indian-American scientist who discovered the limit of the point, when a neutron star becomes a black hole. This could be represented as various stages of neutron star to become a black hole.

4) Beyond this maximum limit the object is said to be sinking in Sp-ti medium. So, there is no object greater than this mass density and thus a finite nature is attained in terms of end point of an evolved object.

5) The sp-ti lines are actually terminating at the edge of the black hole (Fig 57), to be noted which clarifies the misconception that, the space-time is said to be warped inside a black hole, in existing science and technology. For more details refer the book, Fundamental Theory of Singularity (FTS).

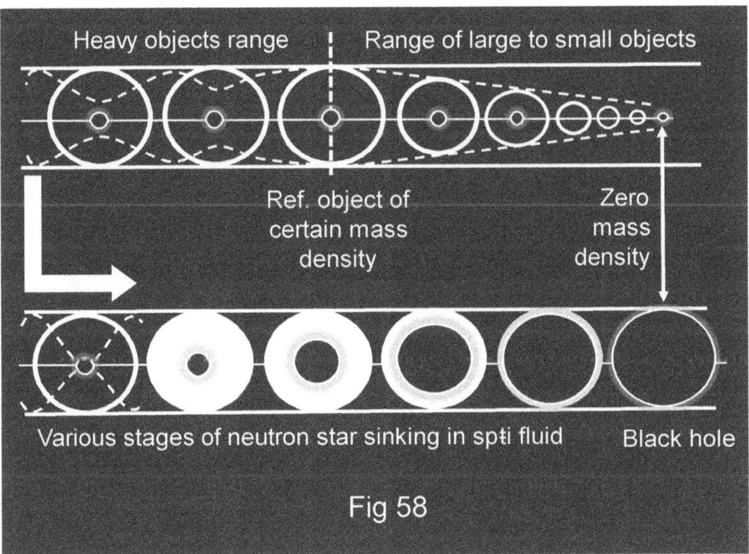

Fig 58

6) The representation shows that, there is a black hole developing from the core, as the object sinks. Now, if the object is said to be sinking in the medium, from where to where? It is sinking from the vacuum medium into the fluid medium. So, the black hole is an identification left behind in the vacuum medium by the sinking object.

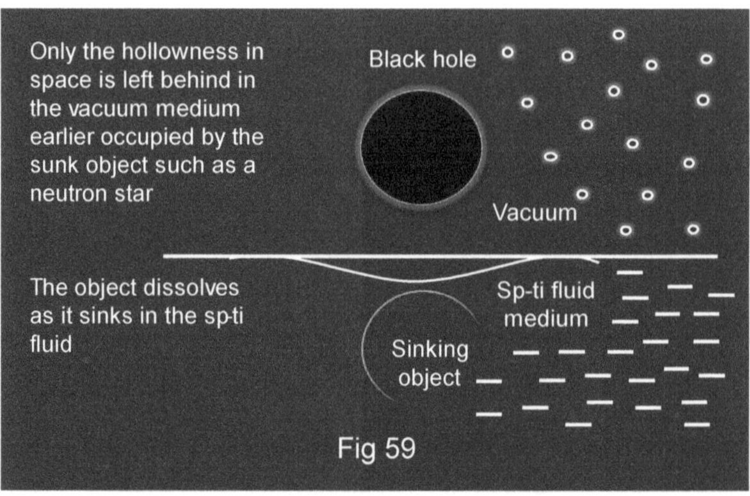

Fig 59

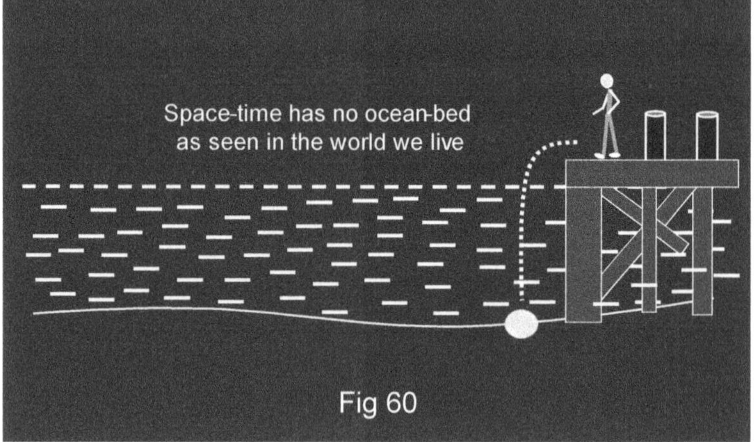

Fig 60

7) Does the object sinking in Sp-ti fluid medium is same as that of an object dropped in the ocean we see in our world? No, the object dropped in the sea water, remains on the floor bed whereas, the object in space-time dissolves and becomes one with the medium as it sinks. Further, as the object does not exist as it enters the fluid medium, we do not require the detail of how deep the sp-ti ocean is and could simply assume that, there is no floor bed for this ocean. Thus, the object crossing the maximum limit i.e., the Sp-ti tolerance max is only the point of beginning of sinking. After which only the black hole is seen in vacuum medium.

8) More than the scientific tools and equipment such as a powerful telescope, the manual representations here are important to track the details. Say for instance, the neutron star after the maximum limit starts to breakdown and it is no more an object with certain shape and it is like a processing matter. However, if it is still had not attained the point of zero mass density or simply zero mass, then in that case, is it possible to track the process inside the black hole? The answer is yes. Again, refer to Fig 58, the developing black hole is surrounded by the reducing mass of the neutron star, if we consider this mass as a sphere inside a black hole, we could track this object under destruction till Sp-ti 0. For this, we simply have to flip the representation between black hole and the reducing mass, as shown in Fig 61.

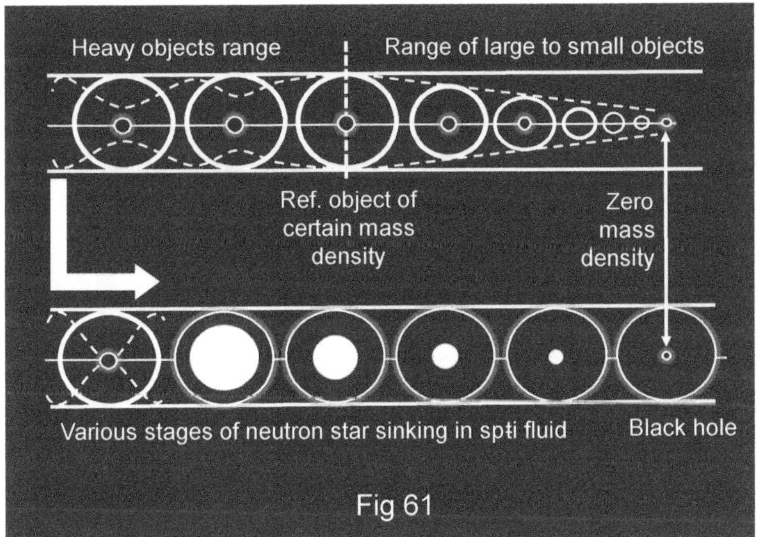

Fig 61

The neutron star after certain limit breaks down itself and the space occupied by it becomes hollow in the medium. If vacuum itself is an empty space then what is the nature of this hollow space formed in it? There are two types of vacuums introduced in FTS, 1) The space where the object can move is called as **spacious vacuum**. 2) The space where the object cannot even enter into it, is called as **absolute vacuum**.

Absolute vacuum is the technical term for black hole. To understand it better, let us consider the representation in Fig 61, where the starting point before the quantum scale and ending point after the macro-scale, in terms of zero mass density remains the same except a difference that, the ending point is surrounded by the hollow space, in general called as black hole.

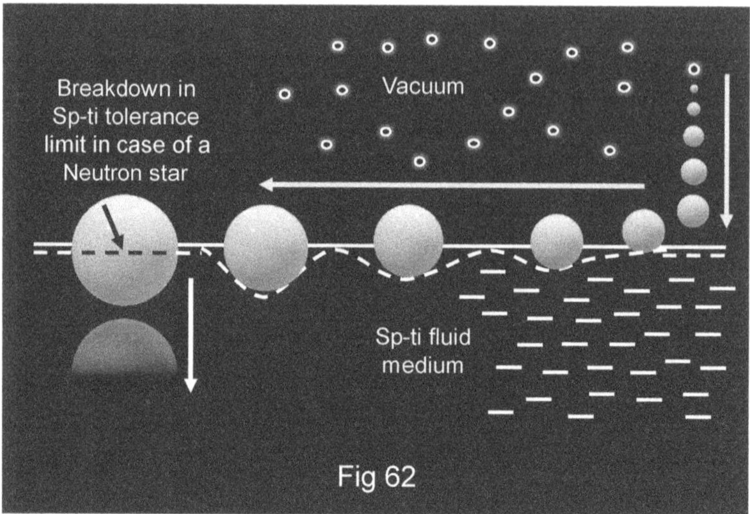

Fig 62

We may think that the zero-mass density point is located at the center of the hole but the fact is, the entire black hole is filled with the absolute vacuum which means it is full of Sp-ti 0s in merged condition and irrespective of the size of the black hole, whether it is small or large, it behaves as a singular point. That's why we said the Sp-ti configuration begin from a point and ends in a point where both the points are the same by nature.

15.0 SP-TI GRID LINES (Vs) GRAVITATIONAL ROPE

We called the sp-ti lines to be a rope network and later said that the rope cannot be bent by the heavy object and indeed has the purpose of tying the object in space-time. Moreover, even the sp-ti lines serving support for the solidity of the object till certain limit, for further increase in mass density of the object it cannot be bending by its own self. So, how to get clarity on the above two cases? What is the real nature of rope of gravitation and sp-ti grid lines? And also, if no bending or curvature then where did elasticity of the medium vanish?

After applying the fluid nature to the medium, the curvature caused by the object is with the tolerance of the fluid medium. The elastic property here is converted into a membrane to insulate the raw nature of the fluid medium from reaching the evolved objects. Means, the elastic nature works like a rubber insulation over the raw liquid and gaseous medium and thus carry the objects on its surface. This insulation is even present as a basic layer coated in the objects such that there is no leakage happens from within the object itself. Refer FTS for the dimensionally hidden Sp-ti ocean, at the background of the Universe. These realities are quite difficult to visualize unless the mind keeps track of the path.

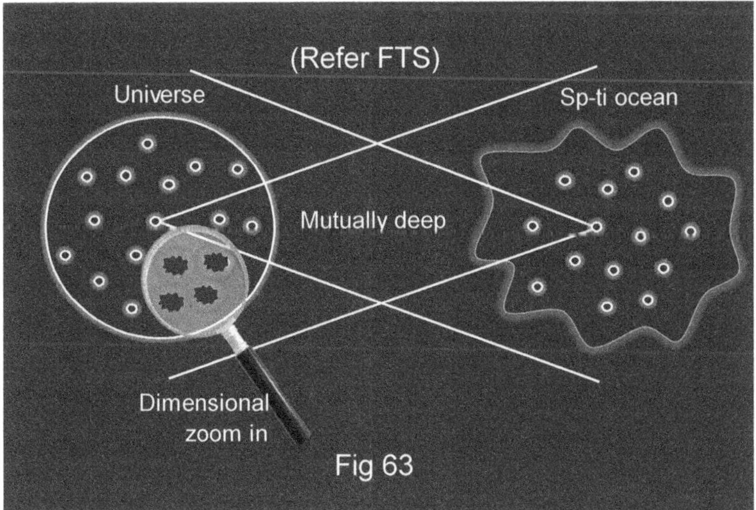

Fig 63

The sp-ti grid lines shall be compared to that of steel rods inside a pillar of the building that serves as the support at the background of the object however, the rope as an accumulated aspect of the overall tensile strength of the membrane could be called as

gravitational rope. FTS explains the Universe we live is just a perception of mind which moves through the Sp-ti frames holding the motion picture of what we see from time to time. So, the rod-like Sp-ti lines have no connections at their ends as in case of the pillars of the building that are actually raised from the foundation. They are only limited to the Sp-ti frames just for solidity of the objects. Gravitational rope could be better understood if represented along with the Sp-ti grid lines. As we know the Sp-ti fabric or membrane have an unchanging thickness, the sp-ti lines associated at this surface level obviously have certain thickness and along with this, the gravitational rope also serves as the reference line for the whole space-time medium, in-spite of both being two different aspects.

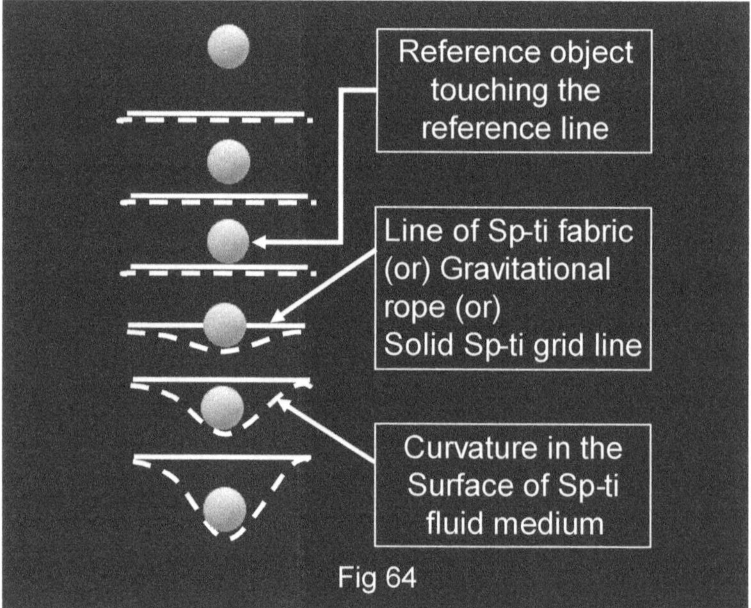

Fig 64 shows, the only change happening is the curvature caused in the surface of Sp-ti fluid medium and the layer of insulation (fabric or membrane), the line of Sp-ti grid and the gravitational rope, all the three serves as the reference line from which the object is positioned as per the mass density value.

Maximum thickness of Sp-ti grid lines constituting the surface of fluid medium
Gravitational rope from surface to depth of the medium through sp-ti grid lines of various thicknesses
Sp-ti 0

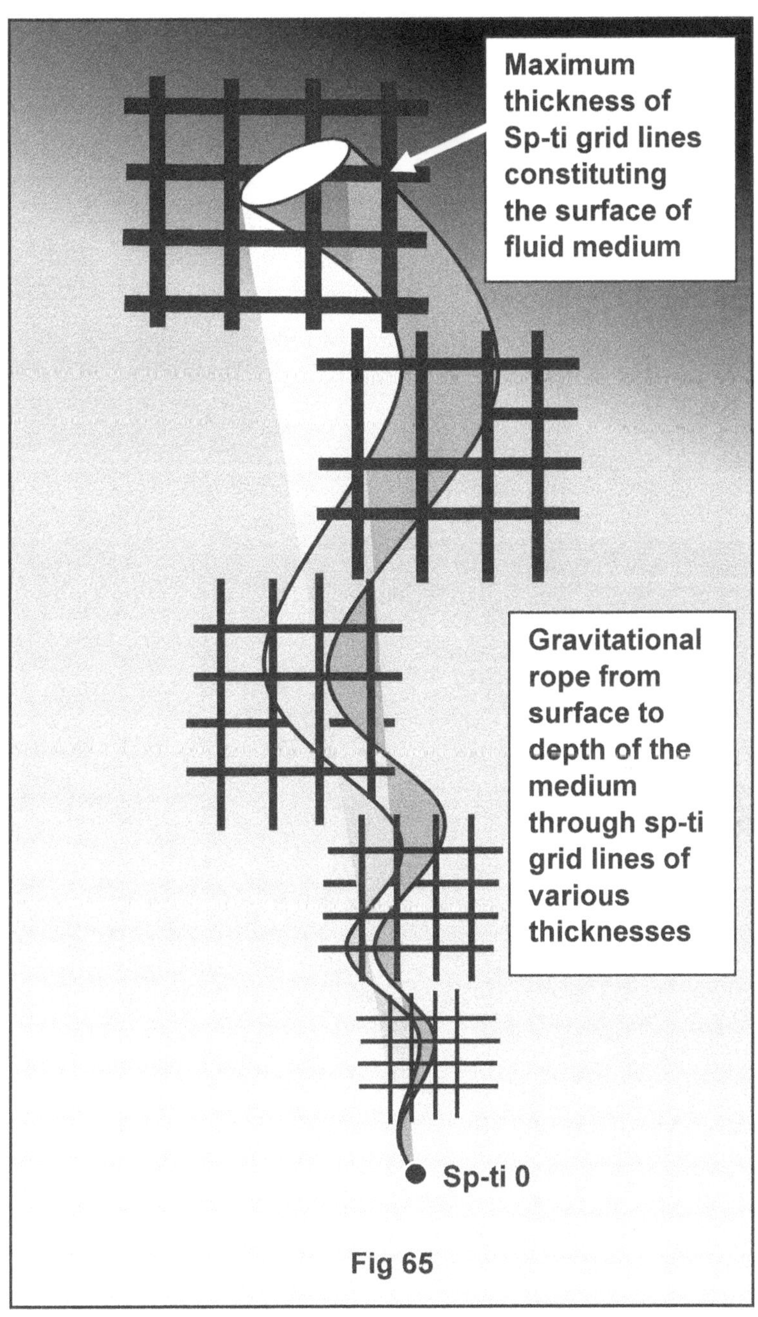

Fig 65

Obviously, the descending less mass density objects detaches away from the line to reach zero mass density or Sp-ti 0 point and the increasing heavy masses curves the surface of fluid medium until the breakdown limit is reached, as in case of the neutron star. Now, let us draw the gravitational rope that begins as a thread growing from Sp-ti 0 till macro-scale through sp-ti grid lines of various thicknesses, as shown in Fig 65. How is the gravitational rope at the surface of the Universe we live or at the Sp-ti fabric level looks? Obviously, it must be a rope of same thickness. To better understand this, we use a method same like the Sp-ti grid configuration, we arrange the objects from macro to quantum scale using gravitational rope to pass through them. Now, if we mark the reference object, it causes a break line in the gravitational rope itself as shown in Fig 66.

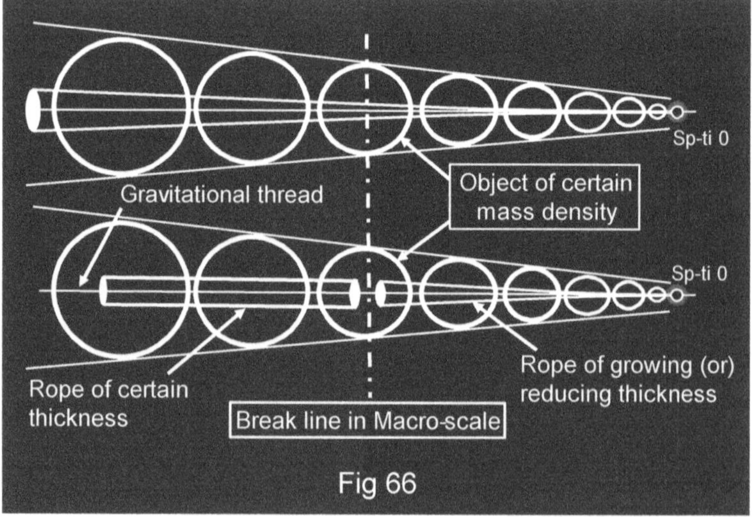

Fig 66

The rope attains certain thickness means it has a finite value and the increasing scale towards infinity is also already solved by applying the fluid nature where two surfaces from above and below are touched by the reference object and the increasing high mass density objects does not exceed in size and remains within these two parallel lines, discussed already. Now, one may ask that the thickness of the rope is solved to be finite however the rope must have a length, if the Universe is expanding then obviously this rope must be infinite, how to solve the same? If we consider a galaxy or a solar system, despite of the Universe expansion they are still bound to be a system about a center. Means, their local reality never changes. In that case the gravitational rope also could be assumed to be around this center point. For that, the rope must be circular and a closed loop to become finite. So, the representation has further changes (Fig 67) where the reducing thickness of the rope could be shown as a tail and the rope of same thickness on either side.

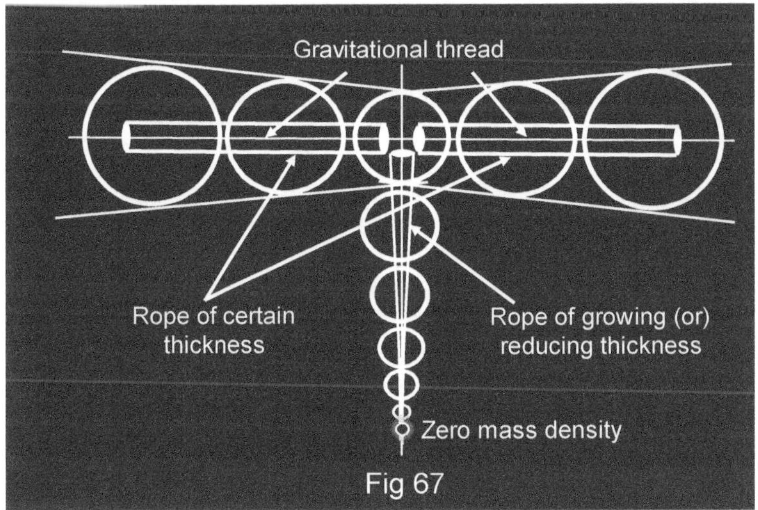

Fig 67

The gravitational rope has a thread at its center which is always connecting all range of objects even though the rope is passing only through the heavy objects of the Universe. The objects of lesser mass density apart from undergoing gravitational effect such as free falling and revolution, they are always connected to these big objects in terms of gravitational thread (Fig 38), is an important note in space-time study. The thickness of gravitational rope need not necessarily be same as the sp-ti grid lines (Fig 39). They are same only in terms of reference line, for the objects positioned pertaining to their mass densities. Fig 47 representation D model is suitable for gravitational rope to be a reference line for less mass density objects.

Gravitational thread
Core points of heavy mass objects
Object of certain mass density
Less mass density objects away from looped G-rope of heavy masses still connected with them through gravitational thread at quantum level.
Zero mass density

Fig 68

Circular rope of same thickness, accumulated and lying top of the surface of the fabric
Gravitational rope Vs Sp-ti grid lines

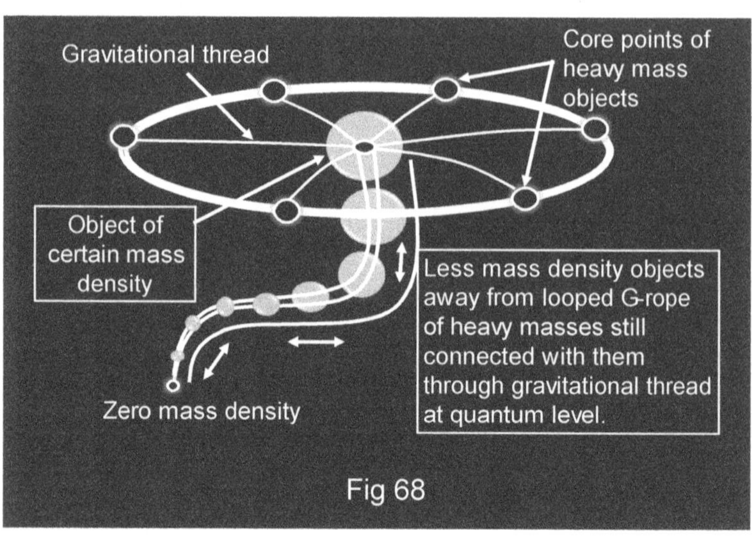

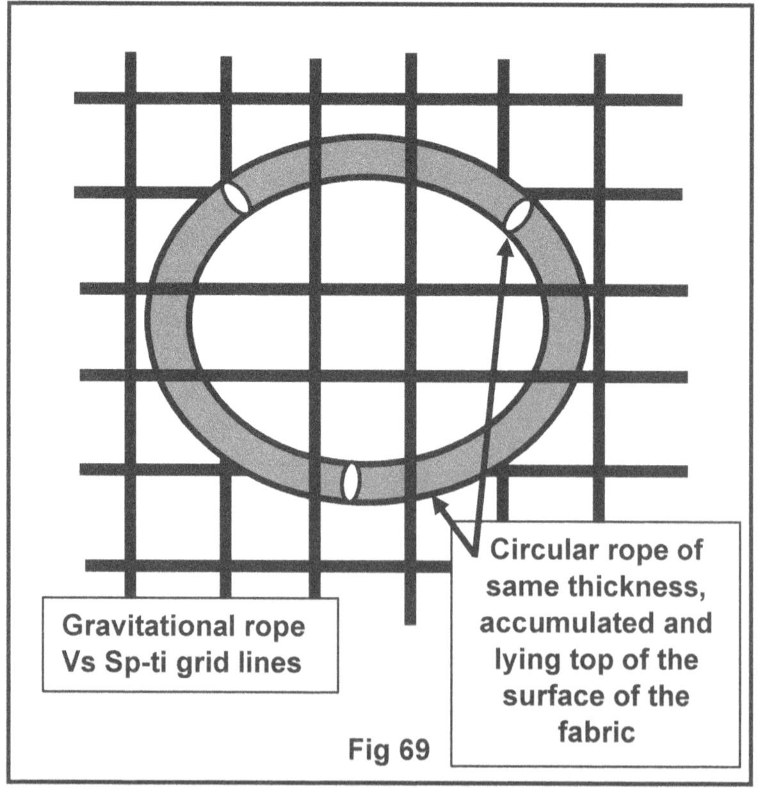

Fig 69

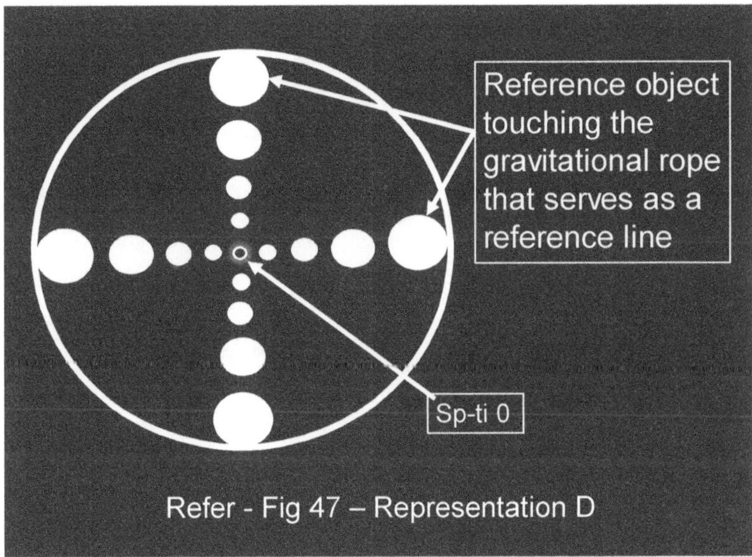

Refer - Fig 47 – Representation D

In continuation with Fig 64, we apply the size factor indicating various mass densities of the objects positioned above and below the gravitational rope as the reference line.

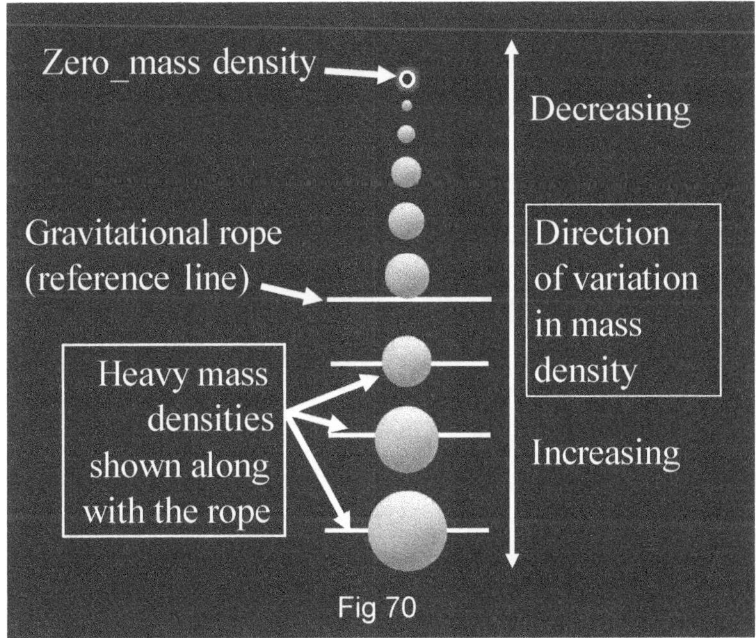

In Fig 70, clearly the less mass densities above reference line are shown with reducing size that reaches the point of zero mass density. And below the reference line, the objects of increasing mass density more than the reference object are shown with increasing size however, what does the rope represented along with the heavy objects means? In Fig 64, the objects of same size are away from the reference line either above or below (note for minute changes). Now, we have already discussed that the gravitational rope passes through the core point of all the heavy mass density objects, which implies the heavy objects minimum touches this rope and at no point they are away from it.

Now it is possible to interpret whether the gravitational rope would break for an object of certain high mass density value or not. Clearly, after applying fluid nature, the gravitational rope would slip out from the heavy object rather than breaking.

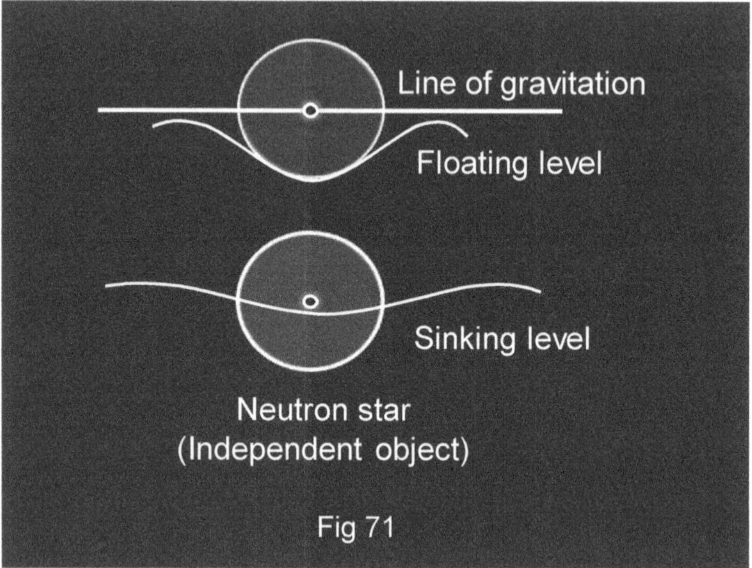

Fig 71

For example, the neutron star has very high mass density and it is not supported by gravitation anymore as it is moving from the limit of a floating object and start to sink in space-time fluid medium. Such objects are said to be independent in nature whereas gravitation is associated with dependency between any two objects (minimum).

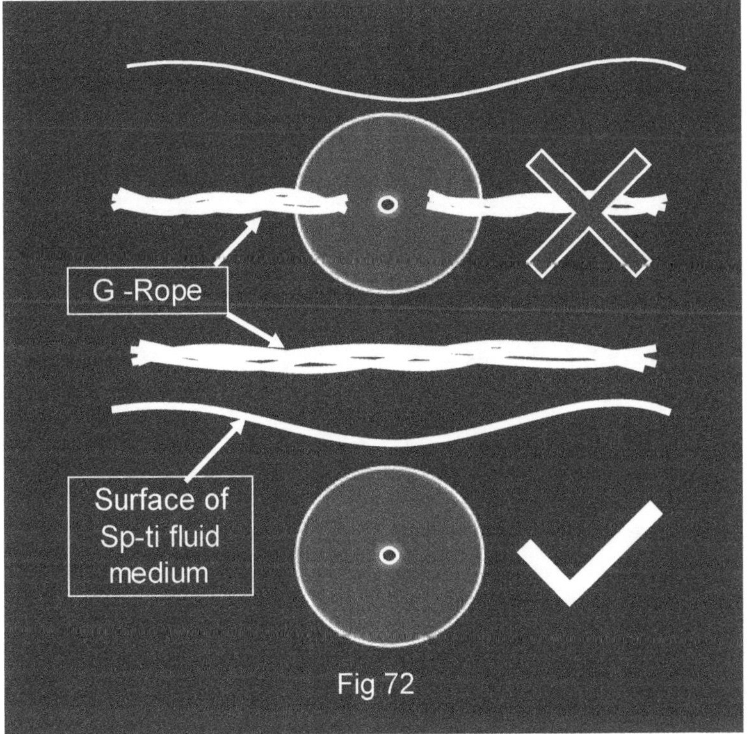

Fig 72 shows, the gravitational rope slips away from the sinking object without a breakdown. It is possible to tie the objects with a rope in our daily life, but how to bind the big objects such as planets in sp-ti medium and that too how come the rope of certain thickness could control the objects of all heavy mass densities in the Universe? We will see some real-time illustrations.

Let us observe a ship tied to an I-beam structure (Fig 73). Here, the rope is not bearing the whole weight of the ship in tons, but the sea water medium does. The rope is just to keep the ship not to move and remain in the destination. Same way the gravitational rope is not bearing the heavy objects but those masses are actually borne by the sp-ti fluid medium itself.

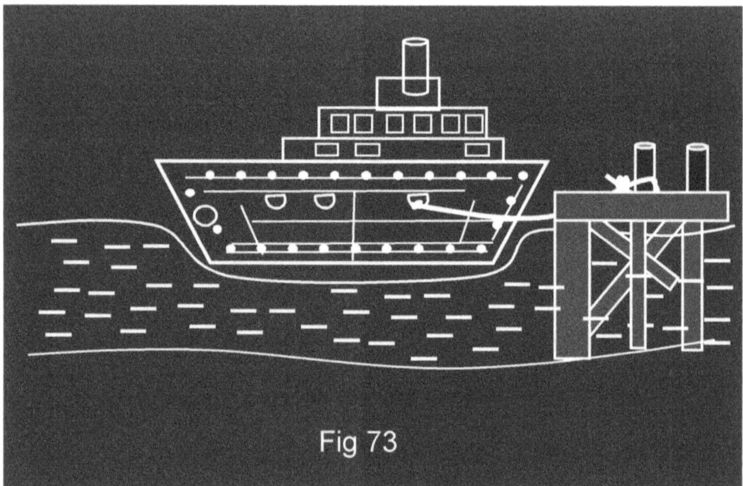

Fig 73

The rope is serving the purpose of controlled motions of the objects but the question is how they are tied?

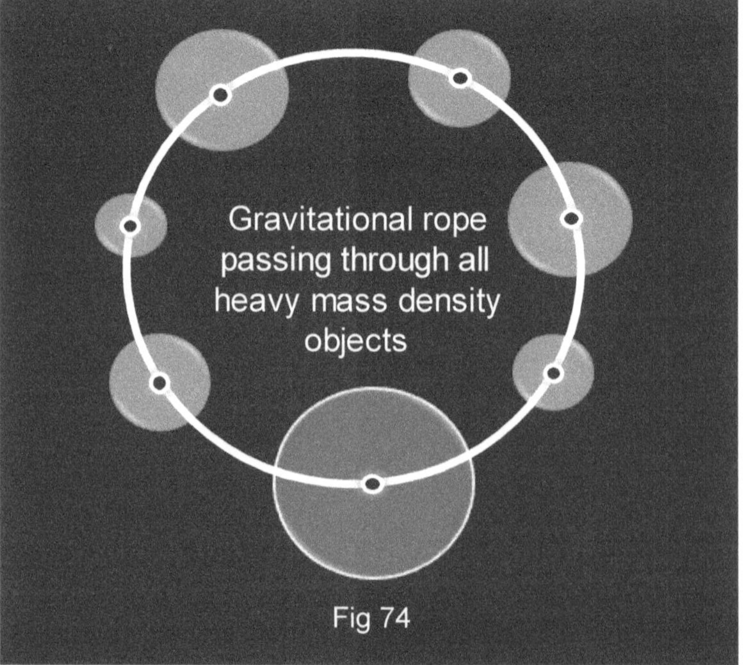

Fig 74

It is absolutely possible, if the rope of gravitation passes through the core of the heavy masses same like beads joined with a thread. Only in this way, the heavy masses would not slip out of the rope and at the same time works in a controlled motion or path.

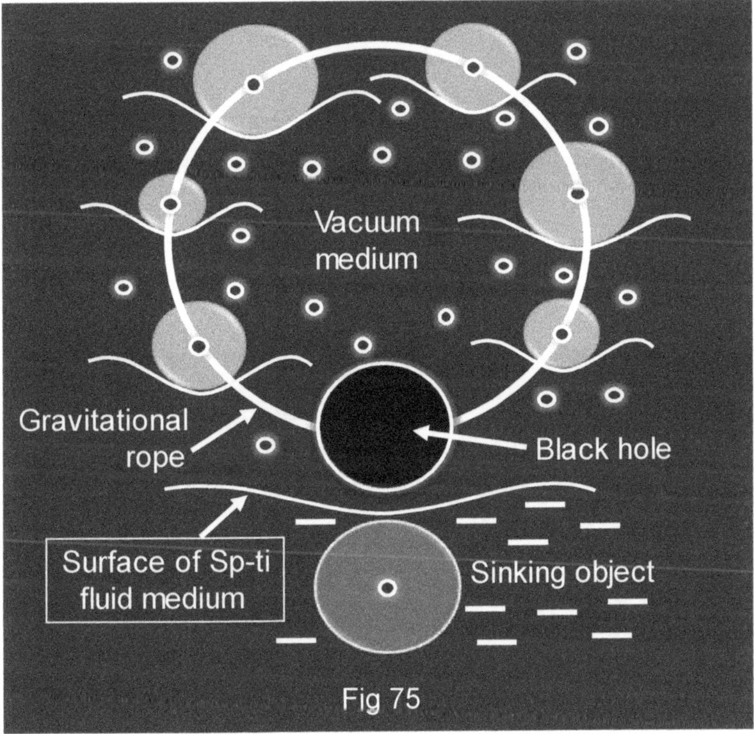

When the mass density is beyond certain limit as in case of a neutron star, the object starts to sink in the medium. As it leaves the rope, it is out of the gravitational loop of objects in the Universe, as shown in Fig 75.

The black hole as already discussed is not forming a steep curve in the medium (Fig 11), instead it forms a ring or a loop in the medium inside which, there is no gravity and even the thread of gravitation terminates at its edge. The basics of black holes shall be discussed in fore coming topics later.

16.0 GRAVITATIONAL WAVES – A MISCONCEPTION IN EXISTING SCIENCE & TECHNOLOGY

Collision of two black holes in space-time is a heavy process during which the ripples are formed in the medium. These waves are said to be a big destructive nature by the scientists that it could rip apart even an entire Universe however, these waves having travelled long distances and on reaching the Earth, it becomes feeble that the devices used to detect these waves shows a negligible reading. These waves are predicted by Sir Einstein as gravitational waves earlier and was confirmed to exist or detected using modern day technology. However, these waves belong to sp-ti fluid medium and at no point gravitation is a wave is our new study. Let us see it with some real-time illustrations.

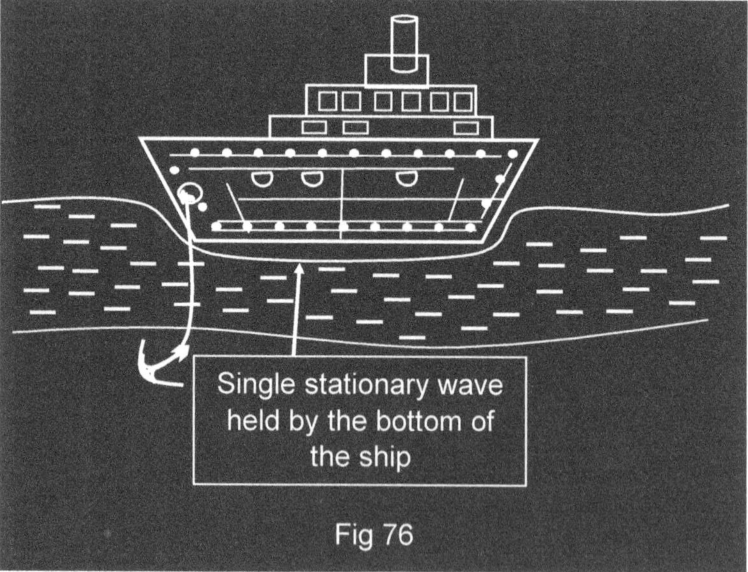

Fig 76

Now, consider a ship stopped by an anchor in the sea. The bottom of the ship presses the surface of water and displaces it with its weight. If the surface of the sea is assumed to be a reference line, then this curvature caused by the ship displacing the sea water could be called as a stationary wave held by the bottom of the ship.

The same is the case with the planets such as the Earth, its mass density curves the surface of sp-ti fluid medium.

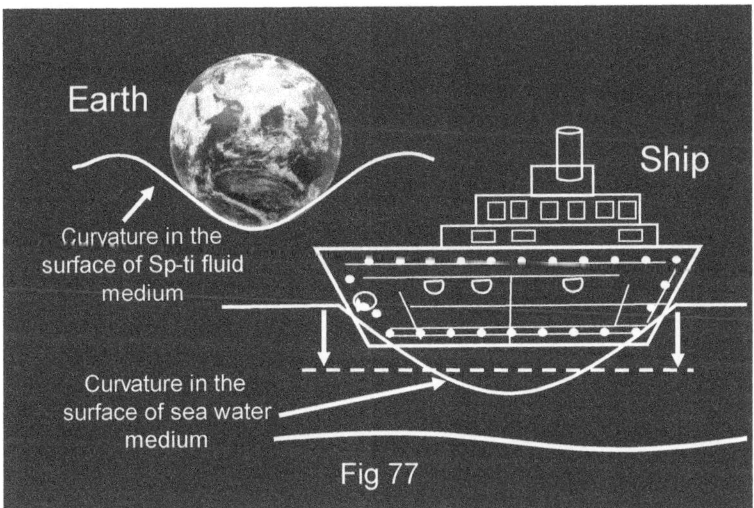

Now, the ripples formed and moved away from the point of two black holes collision, pervades the Universe. These waves hardly reach the Earth or sometimes detected at very small scale. How these waves could be shown to connect with the above said macro-scale stationary wave held by the planet Earth?

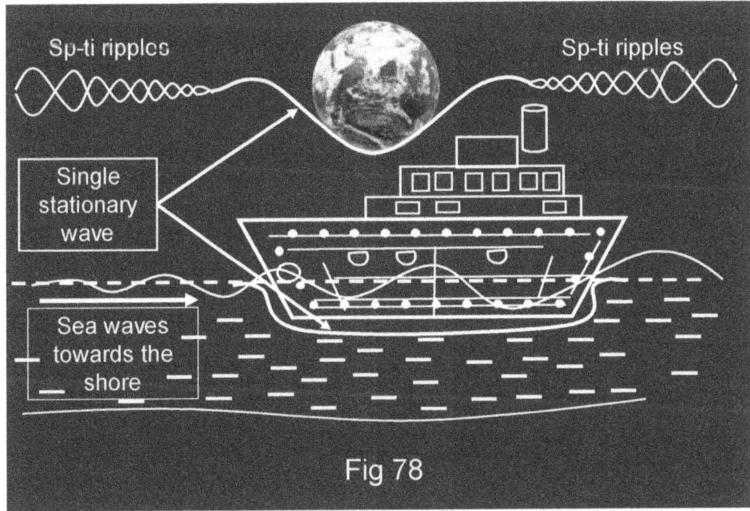

The ship near to the shore holds one big wave and apart from this, there are waves on the surface of the sea that continuously hits the shore. However, in case of sp-ti ocean there is no shore, the waves raising on the surface has to reach a maximum level and again fall and reduce through travelling over distances, become feeble and then attain sp-ti 0. So, it is same like sea waves, it could even add up with the stationary wave based on the consequences or how near some heavy process is happening in the medium.

Thus, the macro-scale stationary wave and the quantum scale rising and falling waves on the surface of the Sp-ti medium shall be represented as uniform increase or decrease in wave.

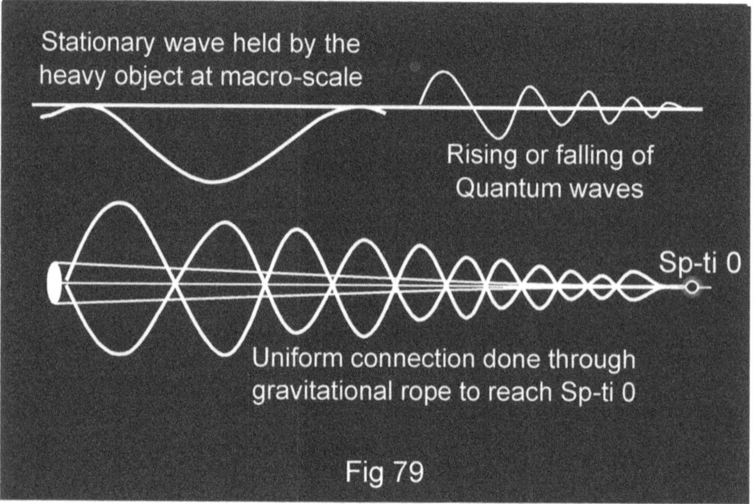

Fig 79

This representation using the rope is mainly to show, at no point gravitation is a wave in Sp-ti medium, as it is assumed in modern science and technology. It is always a line that can be drawn to pass through the axis of the waves, starting from a thread at Sp-ti 0, growing into a thick rope towards macro-scale. The wave nature is always indicating the fluid nature of the sp-ti medium itself.

Now, we shall see the change in Einstein's field equation after applying the fluid nature to the sp-ti medium. Here, the displacement of fluid medium is again accounted in terms of matter and energy as a conversion. The three sections of the equation same as one another, of which fluidity is new to study.

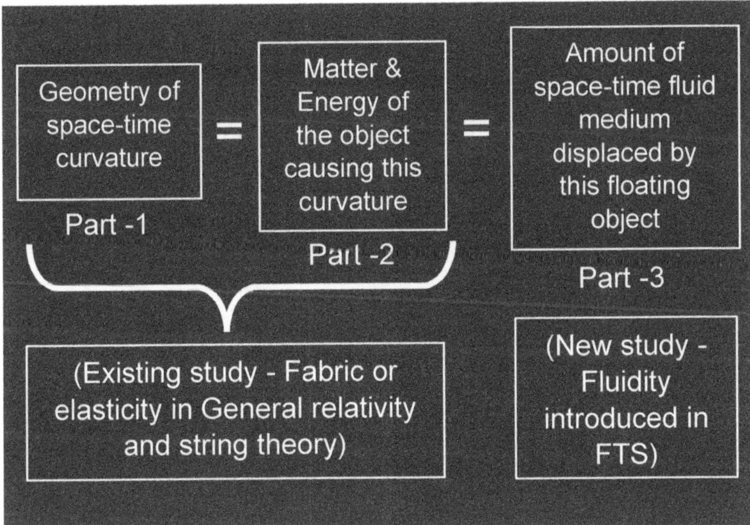

(i) Gravitational rope – at the background of a solar system

As we have discussed already, the length of the gravitational rope is finite. It shall not be assumed to extend along with the expanding Universe but it is a closed loop governing a local reality such as a solar system. Again, we draw a representation in which the rope passes through all the heavy objects of the solar system including Sun in a row.

Here, Sun is not the center of the solar system to be noted. The reference object of certain mass density along with its broken rope whose tail end leads to singularity could be shown at the center of the circular loop.

The complete static representation of gravitation along with the objects from macro-scale to quantum scale and then terminating or emerging at singularity could be shown as in Fig 80. After applying the fluid nature of the medium, the representation alters for a working mechanism.

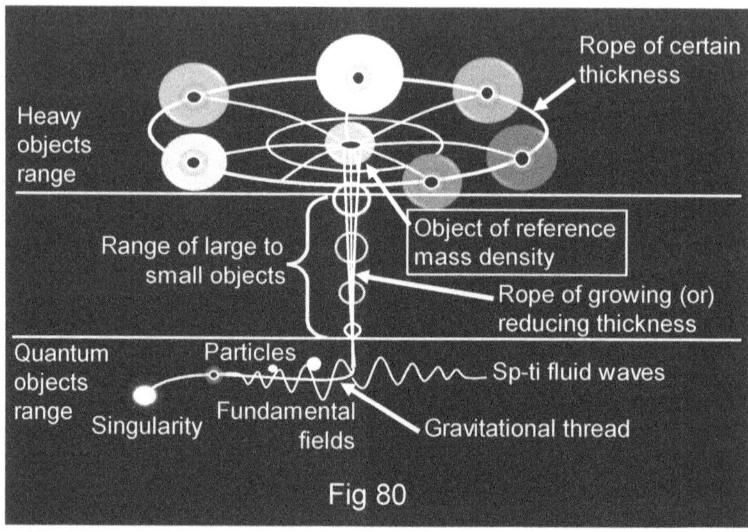

Fig 80

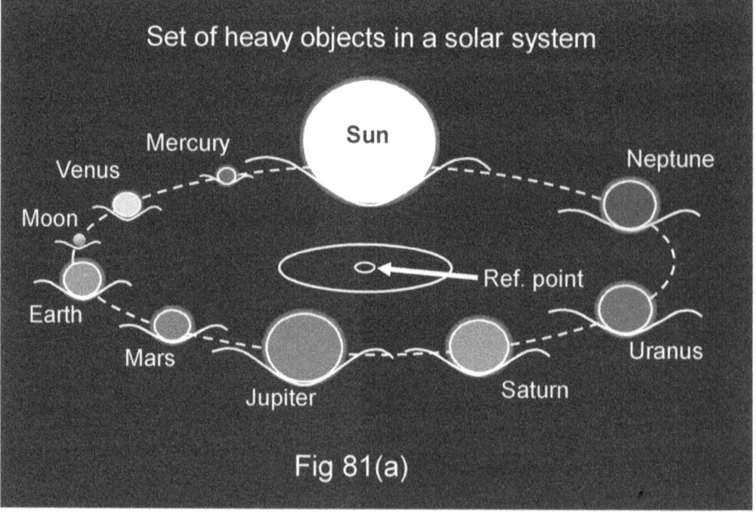

Fig 81(a)

The fluid medium being covered by the membrane, the fluidity bears the mass density of the objects, whereas the liquid proof membrane makes the objects to re-arrange on top of it however, only the Sun comes to the balancing center for all the planets. However, the arrangement of planets is not in the order of increasing or decreasing mass densities. We could assume some randomness in nature and proceed the representations.

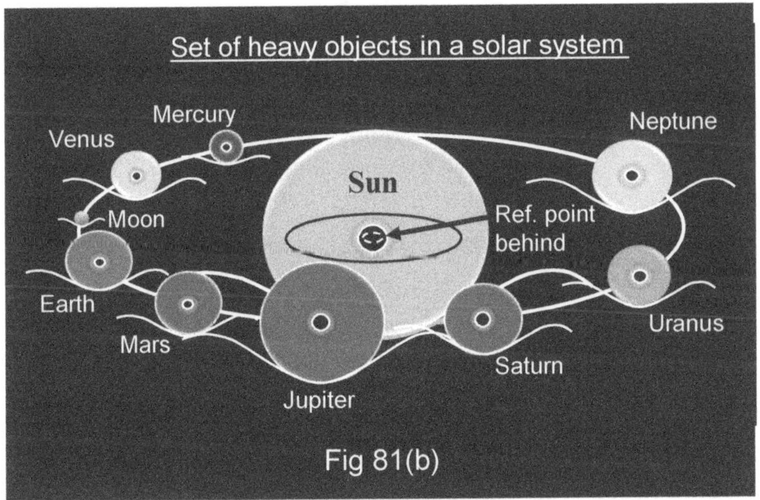

Fig 81(b)

As we know the planets revolve around the sun, each planet is connected to core of the sun through a gravitational loop called as **primal gravitation**.

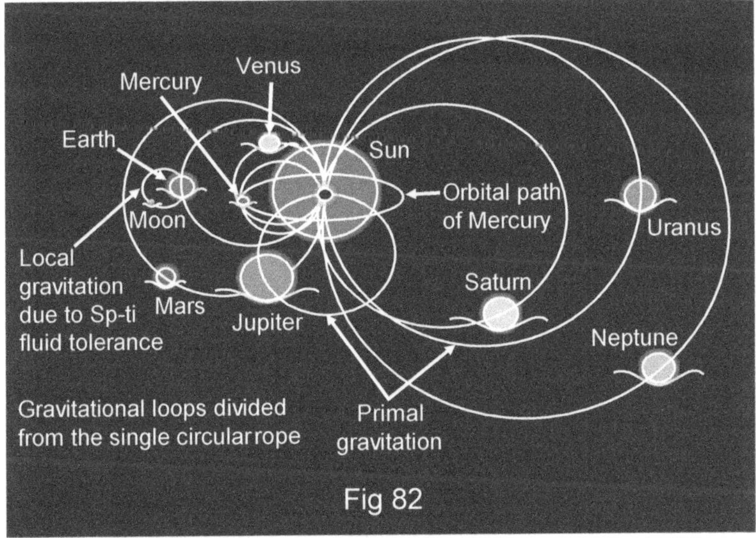

Fig 82

Then every single loop has a path around the sun called orbits. There are further sub-divided loops called as local gravitational loop, in case of moon and the planet. This is due to the difference in tolerance curves by the objects which is same as the Einstein's gravitation model however, it is differentiated in terms of local gravity from primal gravity, as the new study. Once looped by gravitation, the object revolves around the sun. Thus, the path around the Sun is a duality of gravitation called as Orbitation or orbital path for the planetary motion, Fig 83.

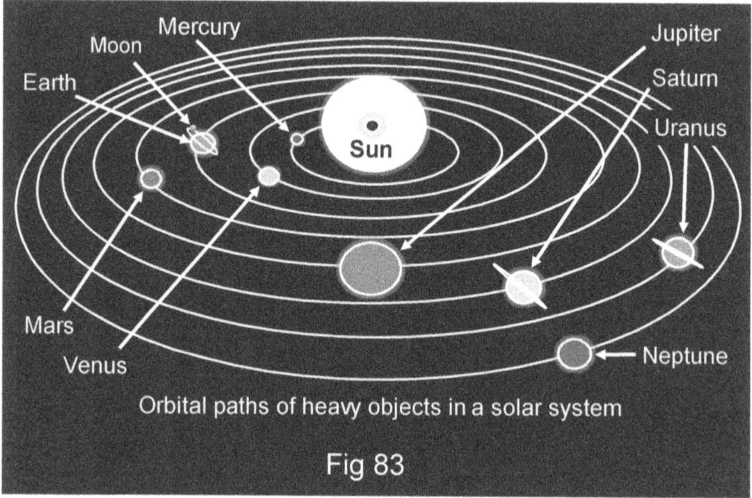

Now, we will come back to the representation of space-time fabric in the existing studies to see how it is modified after applying the fluid nature. Sir Einstein tried to simplify gravitation with one mass causing the curvature in fabric and derived a field equation. But FTS shows general relativity to be a duality that when there is a cause for gravitation its effect could not be neglected.

Thus, the singular perspective is applied for further analysis of sp-ti fabric and revealed the new study of gravitation along with the fluid nature of space-time medium. The FTS also clearly explains how gravitation network works only with sp-ti 0 points throughout the existence, even without object and thus, it is independent of mass. Means, mass is required only for a physical understanding. And even in that case, it is not one or two masses as said by

Newton or Einstein but properly need three different masses to demonstrate gravitation at surface level as follows.

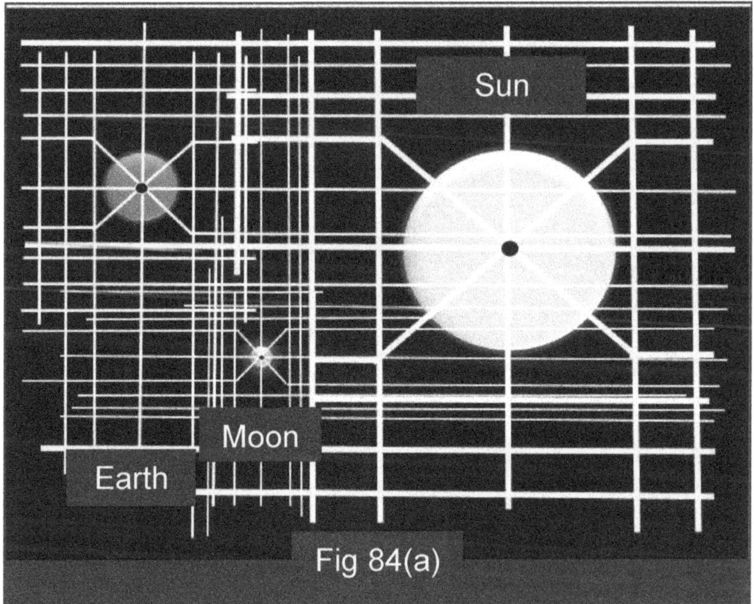

Fig 84(a)

Even the moon has a direct loop with the sun and has the influence called primal gravity however, it is more attracted towards the Earth due to the difference in Sp-ti tolerance curve which causes a local gravity stronger than the primal gravity. So, there is a great orbit available for moon around Sun besides its local orbit around the Earth, to be noted.

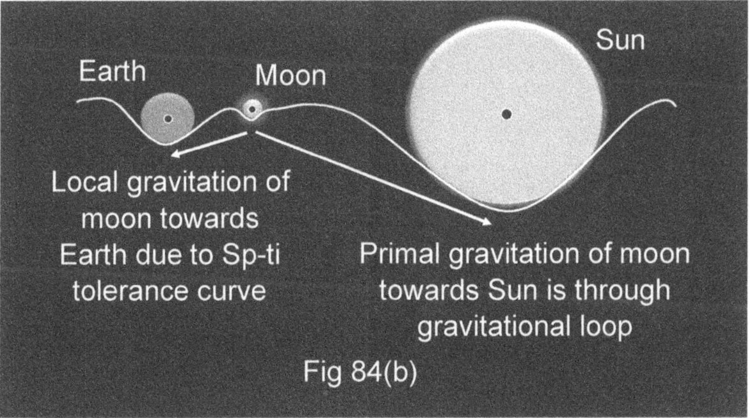

Fig 84(b)

The gravitation here fundamentally works with three sp-ti 0 points with different surface or depth levels.

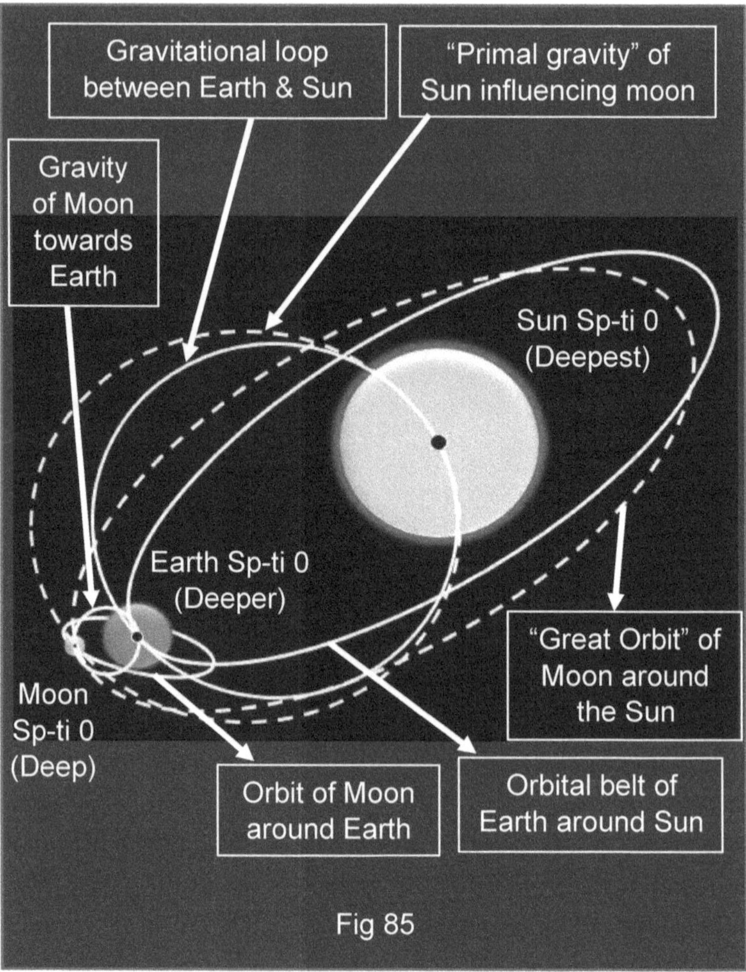

Fig 85

This gravitation model is more or less same as Sir Einstein's representation. However, relativity did not cross the limit of sp-ti fabric and derived a field equation only at the surface level. FTS has revealed the fluidity covered by this elastic membrane and have shown the sp-ti ocean to exist beneath this fabric hidden behind three real dimensions. Thus, the working of gravitation even without the masses is newly introduced to studies.

Also, quantum thread of gravitation is connecting all the objects of the Universe at the depth of sp-ti medium whereas the gravitational rope is governing the macro-scale objects only.

(ii) Tree diagram of Gravitation:

The gravitational rope is circular and perhaps have a disconnection among the solar systems or galaxies and have different roots towards singularity. Thus, a tree diagram is shown in FTS.

The reference object we used in our representations is ideal. It has no reason for its motion due to any differences caused in Sp-ti medium so, this fixed object of certain mass density shall be shown to be contained within the sun. This inclusion has a main purpose that, the reference object holds the tail end of gravitational rope reaching to singularity. So, the figure of gravitation is almost same like a tree that has trunk, branches, sub branches and root.

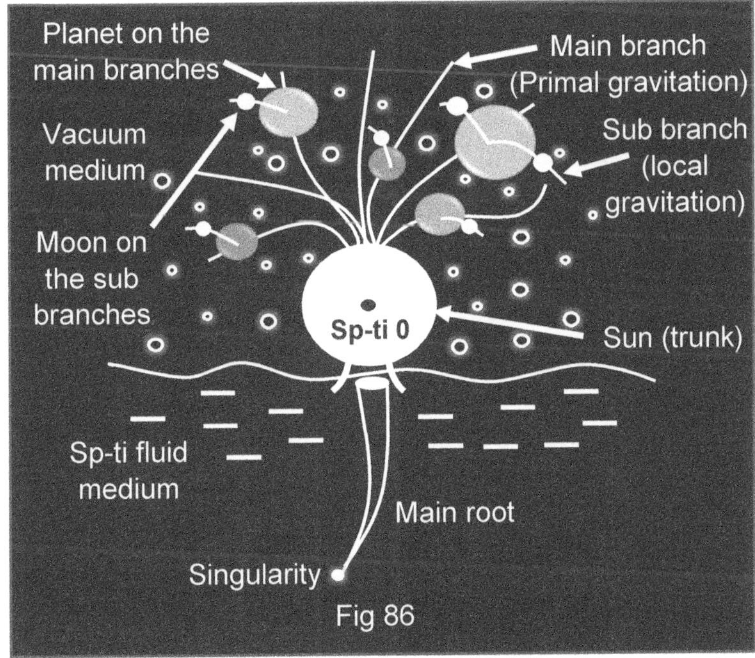

Fig 86

The gravitation at its deepest nature are the **channels to conduct the forces** and does not mean to be any force, as it is believed in existing science. Gravitational rope to gravitational thread has external effects with objects whereas the cross section of the thread behaves like **miniscule conduits** for the very internal cyclic flow of the sp-ti medium.

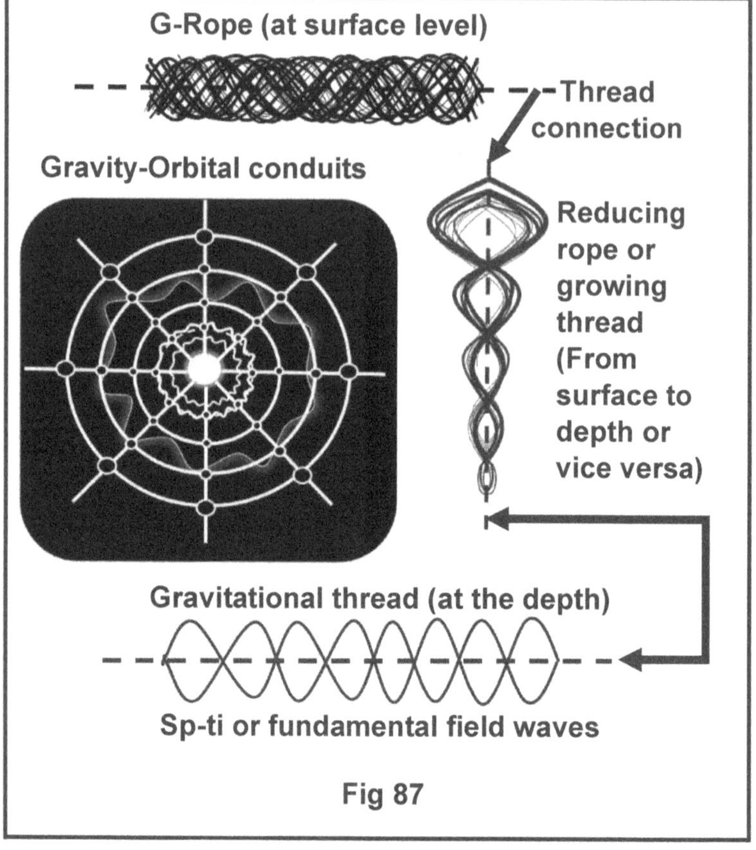

Fig 87

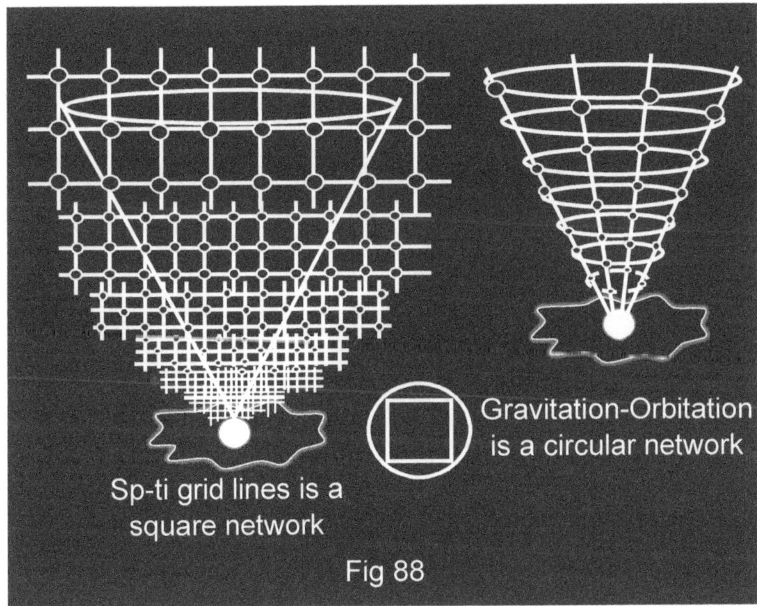

(iii) Working of Sp-ti fluid medium:

Now we move onto the working of the Sp-ti fluid medium after a clear idea about how absolute vacuum was misinterpreted as black holes in existing study.

Referring to the dimensional cone Fig 27, we reduce the sizes of the layers such as absolute vacuum to be deeper and Sp-ti liquid to be deepest. However, according to FTS, when we access the region of absolute vacuum it becomes huge leaving the previous one (spacious vacuum) to be at a reduced scale (Refer-Fig 63).

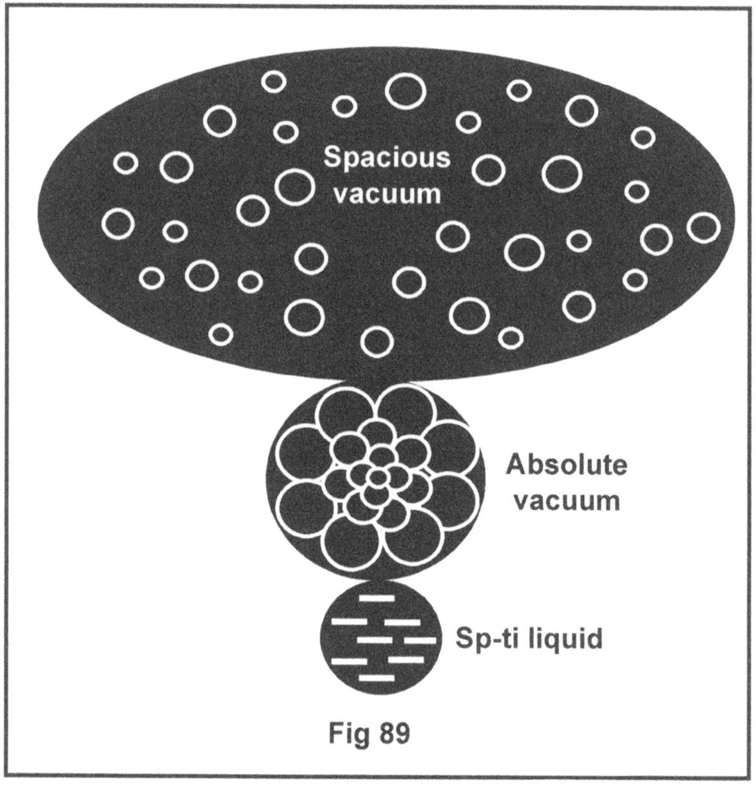

Fig 89

The two lines of the absolute vacuum region is the tolerance limit for the heavy objects to cause curvature in the medium or breakdown of the same beyond certain limits as in case of a neutron star, Fig 90(b). This layer of the absolute vacuum is spread like a membrane and has a tensile strength to bear the heavy objects. We have seen that the less mass density objects are away from this membrane (reference line). And the gravitational rope is an accumulated aspect over the membrane to tie or loop the heavy objects for their controlled motions.

The liquid medium is completely hidden by dimensions but absolute vacuum is deeper rather than a hidden nature, as the heavy objects could touch it and because of which, the gravitational effect is felt on the macro-scale. Now, one may ask if the quantum gravity really exists or not. The answer is yes. As we discussed in the introduction part that gravitation is a bi-directional channel that conducts a downward flow which is about the mass and the upward flow, is carried out by the medium itself.

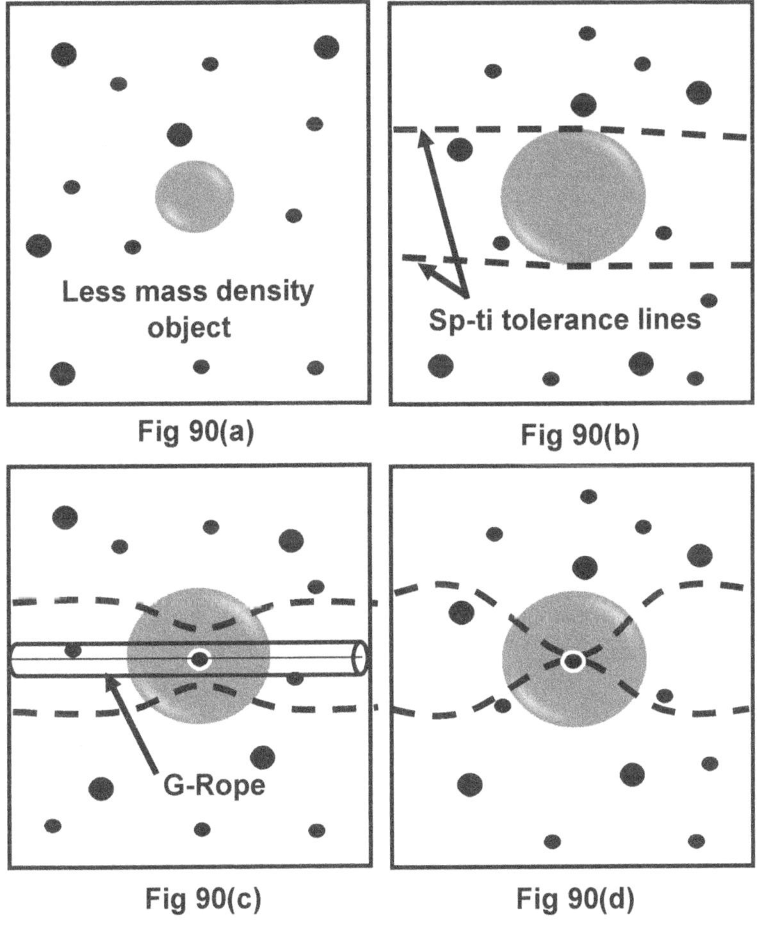

Fig 90(a)

Fig 90(b)

Fig 90(c)

Fig 90(d)

This is what happens at macro-scale such that the level difference between the two curvatures caused by the two different heavy mass densities, with which arrow of gravitation is downward. It is towards the ground for free falling object such as an apple and a higher to lower potential for a revolving object such as a moon.

However, according to FTS the gravitation is concerned about three Sp-ti 0s positioned at three different levels of depth or surface. It is not concerned about the distance at all. In case of a solar system, even though the depth of curvatures is responsible for gravitation, the distance between the curves also accounted. This is the difference between gravitation at macro-scale and quantum gravity. Means, the distance is an extra factor more than the actual requirement and gravitation works even without it. The quantum gravity shall work in a space-time region as an evolution process where the heavy objects and the gravitational rope are not available to access the tolerance limits of the medium, means space would be deeper.

Now, where is the upward flow through gravitational channel could be seen? It is nothing but the creation of objects starting from the fundamental particles such as protons, neutron and electrons to atoms, molecules, elements and compounds and their re-combination to form objects in the Sp-ti medium which are all pushed away from the point of evolution or singularity by space wheels. Even the expansion or contraction of Universe is happening through the gravitational channels driven by space wheels.

17.0 GRAVITATIONAL FILTERS AND STOPPERS

The structure of the black hole filled with absolute vacuum shows that sp-ti 0s are merged one within the other and tightly packed dimensionally and behaves like a leak proof membrane. However, due to the networks such as gravitation-orbitation (circular) for cyclic flow of the medium and Sp-ti grid (Square) for evolution of objects are everywhere.

So, there is a possibility of fluid leak to affect the objects both externally and internally which could be blocked by gravitational stoppers. The waves of the sp-ti ocean that could collapse the object are tapped to minimize the effect by gravitational base filters. For this, we make use of the real dimensions of space-time as it would be unimaginable otherwise.

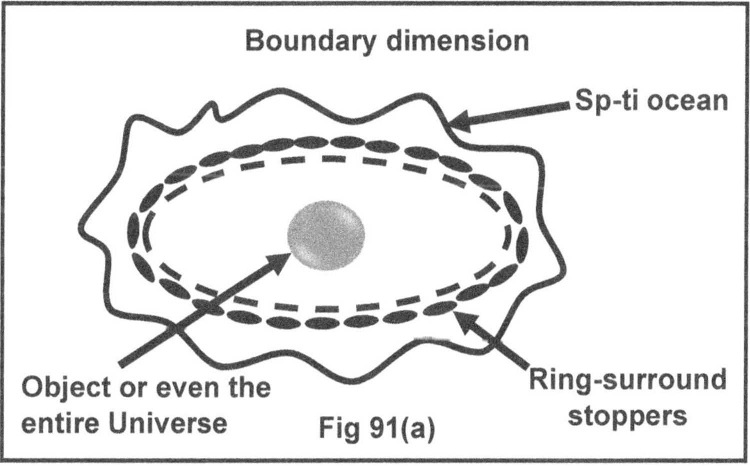

1) The ring-surround stoppers due to boundary dimension surrounding the Universe is same like an island surrounded by the water where there is a shore to stop the waves with its elevation. In case of Sp-ti medium the material that makes the stoppers is the absolute vacuum which works like a rubber cork.

It is also possible for the liquid entry into the Universe, if the heavy objects are not tied with the gravitational rope. The rope makes the Sp-ti bubble of a single object to be extended such that even the whole Universe behaves as one object within the bubble. So, the edge of the bubble protected by these stoppers could feel the waves of the Sp-ti ocean.

2) The base filter are as shown in Fig 91(b). When we consider the base dimension, it is obvious that the base like a plate, has a boundary. So, it is a base-boundary filter. There are two types of filters such as macro and micro base filter to tap the smaller to bigger waves and make it feeble not to afffect the evolved objects of the Universe. The Base is more prominently serves as a filter rather than a stopper.

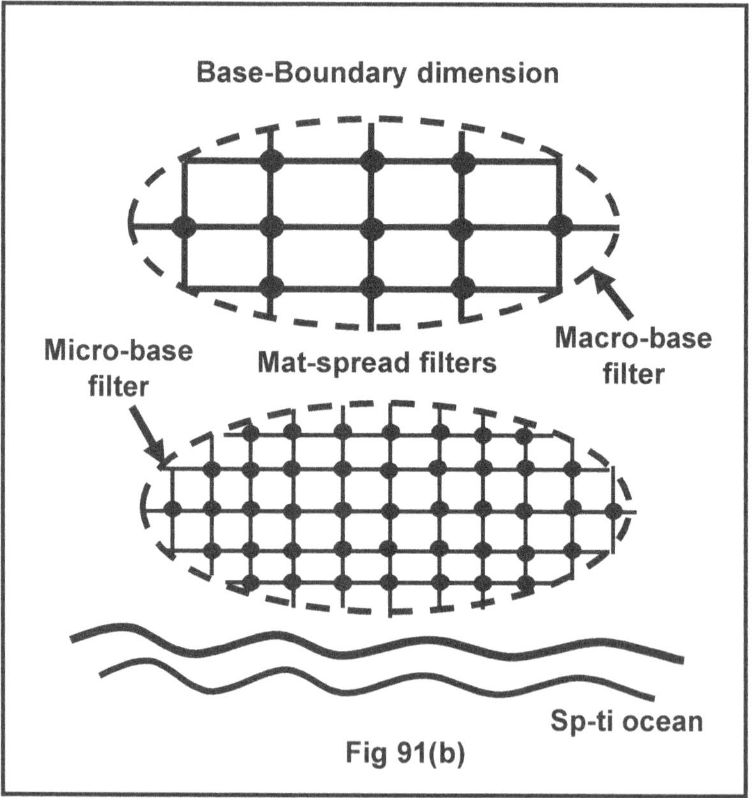

Fig 91(b)

So, the base dimension serves as filters for tapping the rising waves of the Sp-ti ocean due to disturbances. For this reason, the waves arised due to the collision of two black holes, on reaching the Earth becomes feeble or read at negligible scale.

3) Now, boundary can be drawn without base, but base includes the boundary. Further, when core dimension is involved, then everywhere it is core, as all the points are basically core. This is same like a line that connects two points however the line itself is made up of numerous points in a row. The core dimension serves as needle point stoppers as shown in Fig 91(c), where the sp-ti liquid tries to pierce the object in every possible way.

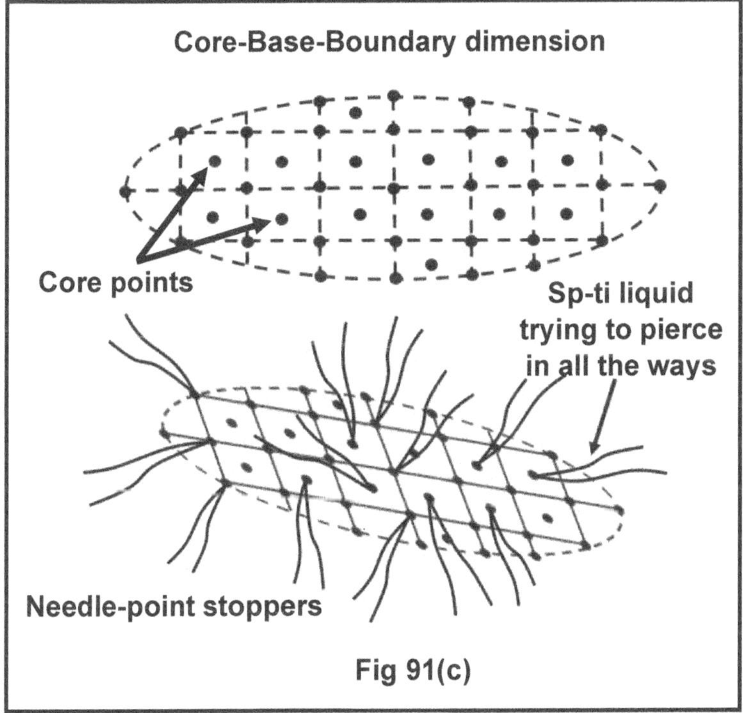

Fig 91(c)

One may ask, why would we even require base and boundary filters or stoppers which could be simply replaced by core points? We separate the features to be base, boundary and core because base-boundary is external and core is internal. Nobody could see this line of separation and it is a very minute technical understanding that needle point stoppers prevent the leak of the Sp-ti fluid to occur from within the object itself and collapse it.

18.0 REAL-TIME UNDERSTANDING OF SP-TI MEDIUM

Sp-ti medium is like a closed water tank with a fountain mechanism that has a circulation pump.

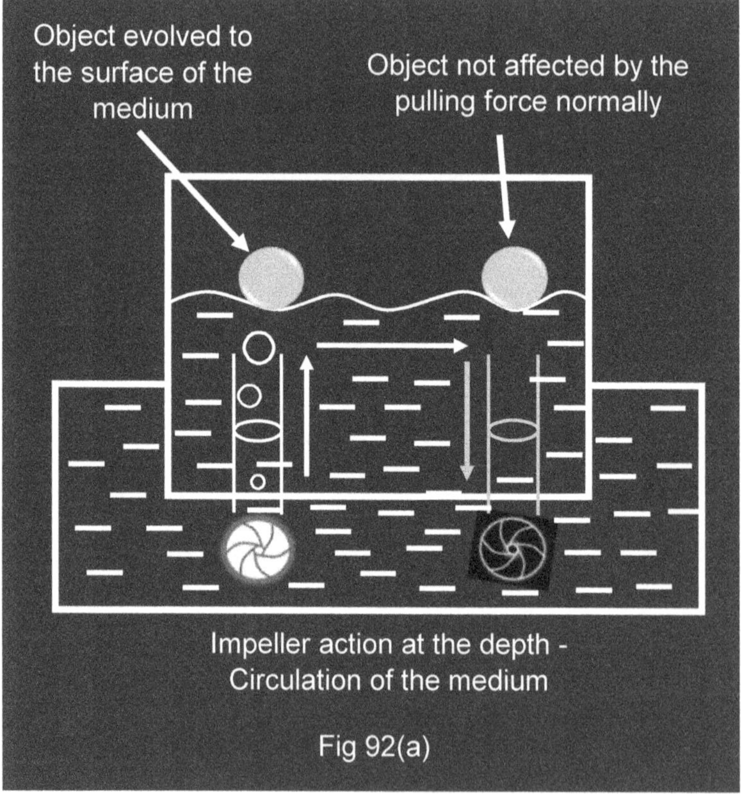

Fig 92(a)

The impeller action at the depth of the Sp-ti medium normally pushes the flow of the medium whose force could also push for creation of objects. The Fig 92(a) shows the particles to evolve like bubbles and become a solid object. Once the macro-objects are on the surface, they are still subjected to the pushing force of the impeller for its sustainment however, the object is normally not affected by the pulling force of the impeller. Means, the pulling face by default draws the medium flow for circulation. The channels responsible for creation and destruction could be extended or reduced depending upon the intensity of the process required. Now, there are two cases for an object to be pulled by the impeller force.

i) Either the channel to be approaching towards the surface, close to the object. ii) Or the object must come to the stage to sink in the medium which would be assisted by the pulling force (as in case of a neutron star).

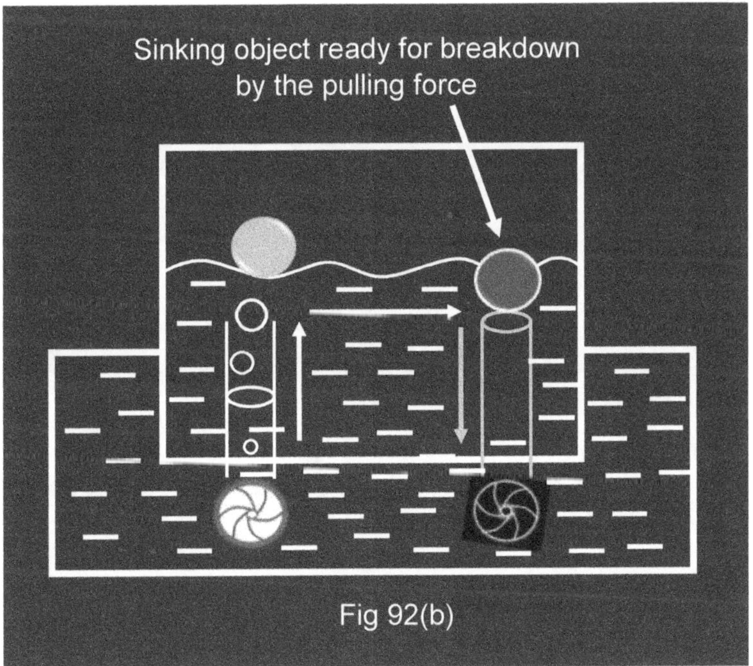

Fig 92(b)

As discussed earlier, self-destruction of an object due to the pulling force is different from the same force destroying the nearby objects. As we said there is no single black hole performing this and it is just an appearance like a giant wheel in 0D. However, for representation purpose the wheel is the appropriate one.

Here, the tank wall structure is made of absolute vacuum as required for the process. The gravitational channels are useful for internal flow of the medium and serve paths for construction & destruction processes as well.

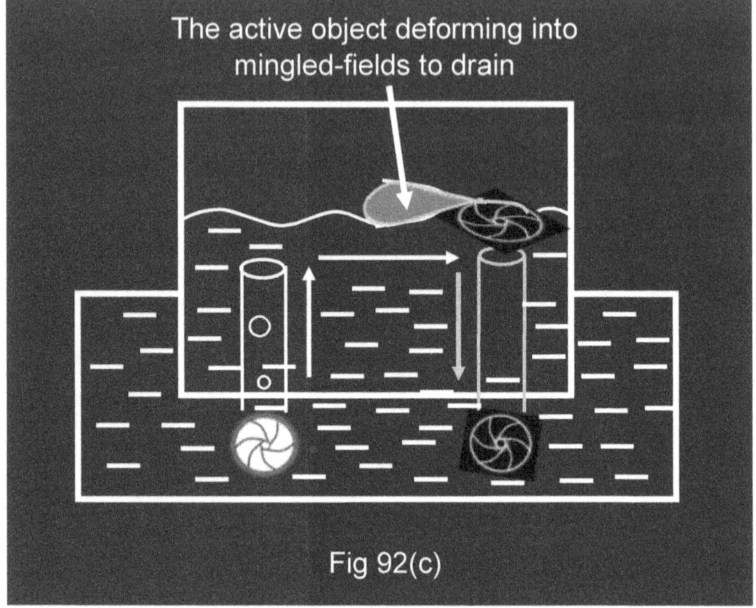

Fig 92(c)

Let us visualize the evolution of object through fundamental field and destruction in the form of mingled-fields in reality as shown in Fig 93. The absolute vacuum containing the Sp-ti 0s could be assume to be settled normally and the grid raises as the impellers work. The fundamental fields find grip to climb through the grid like creepers. Thus, it is represented vertical to the Sp-ti waves. The particle evolves out of the field which on further combination with other particles becomes atoms & elements which then becomes small to large objects.

Fig 93(a) shows the object of certain mass density indicated by certain thickness of the Sp-ti grid. The mingled-fields are not undergoing any separation like the particles drain to their respective fields thus it is drained in mixed form. The time wheel stirs the medium to allow the draining through the grid Fig 93(b).

Macro-scale object with its own Sp-ti grid whose thickness of lines indicates its mass density
Particle evolved from its fundamental field
Unstirred or settled Absolute vacuum
Common grid
Sp-ti waves

Fig 93(a & b)

Active star deforming into mingled-fields flooding along the common grid eventually draining towards singularity

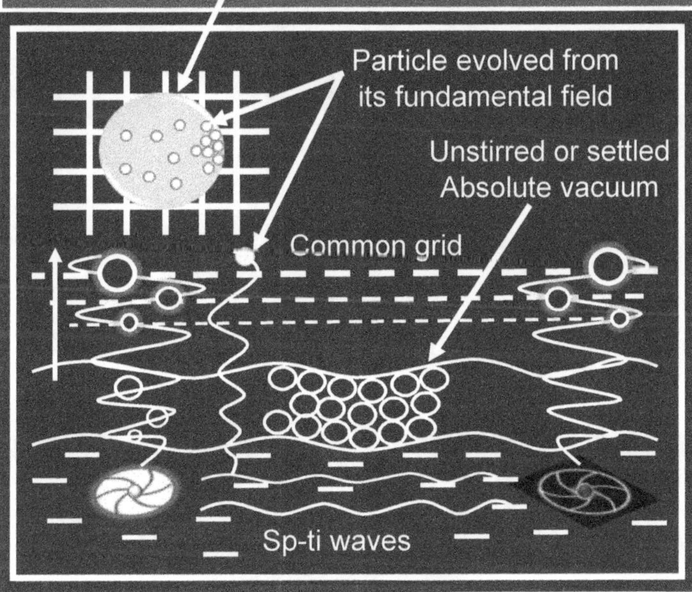

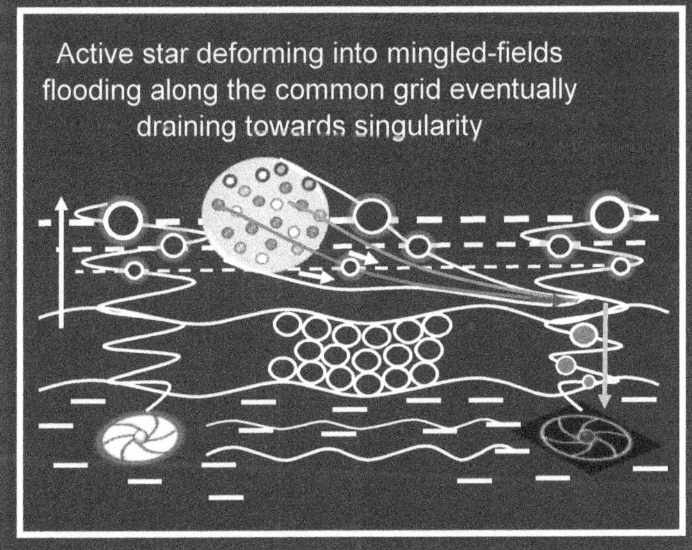

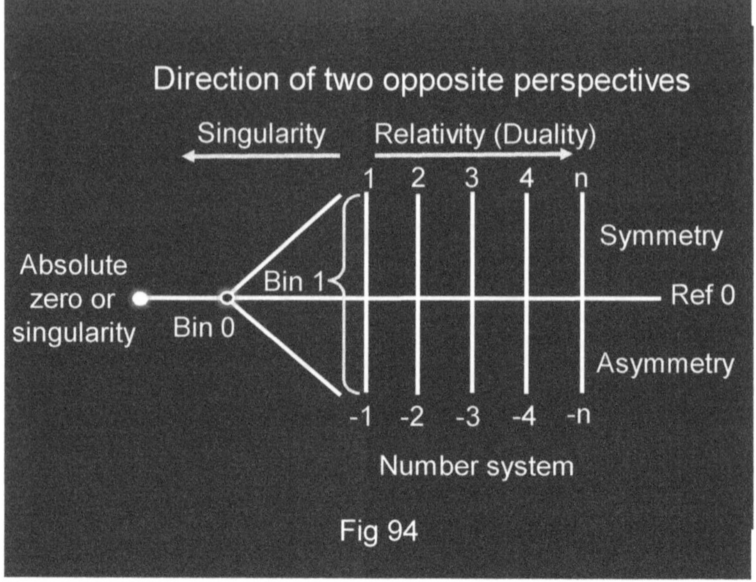

FTS shows how space-time is finite (refer to the book), which means the infinity is not about some countless number but associated with some repetition in a cyclic format. From Fig 94, eventhough the number system arises from singularity, based on the perspective it is pertaining to the relativity(duality) as +n & -n, symmetry-Asymmetry and so on whose dulaity is seperated by reference zero. All the numbers including reference 0 is basically containing binary one such that the system arises only with a direction in which the number shall have an increasing or decreasing count as 1(1), 2(1), 3(1)… Now, what does the binary 0 means?

It is the absence of consciousness or appearance however, indicates the space-time medium to exist still. Then, the absolute zero or singulairty means the absence of medium itself or simply nothing. Further 1 divided by 0 is equal to infinity clearly shows that the number zero is never visualized in reality whereas FTS shows three kinds of zeros each to be unique and new to studies. Infinity in space-time is about the cyclic flow or fountain type mechanism. The infinity has the minimum value of binary one.

The reference zero of number system also basically holds the value of binary one. So when it comes to 1 divided by 0, binary one being deeper than reference zero, the calculation shall be taken as 1 divide by 1 which is equal to one in reality.

1) Number system – 1(1), 2(1), 3(1),…. Where basically 1 represents the binary one which means the appearance.
2) Any number say 1 divided by 0, here the zero is nothing but reference 0 which could be substituted with binary one to save the calculation not resulting to infinity.
3) Now, coming to binary zero, it is deeper than binary one. Bin 0 means the empty space-time medium without objects (mattter & energy) in it.
4) Absolute zero is the deepest where even the sp-ti medium is absent or zero.
5) Symmetry-Asymmetry is one of the basic dualtiies in the existence.

REFERENCES

Self-published my book, titled: "Fundamental Theory of Singularity; FTS" – Year of publishing _2024.

Available in online stores – Notion press, Amazon, Flipkart etc.

----

[1] Self-reference_13: New Theory of Gravitation – Based on Fundamental Theory of Singularity (FTS). [Volume 12, Issue 01, 2025]. (IJARPS –www.arcjournals.org).

[2] Self-reference_12: Fundamental Theory of Singularity; Formulated study – 3. [Volume 11, Issue 01, 2024]. (IJARPS –www.arcjournals.org).

[3] Self-reference_11: Fundamental Theory of Singularity; Formulated study – 2. [Volume 10, Issue 10, 2023]. (IJARPS –www.arcjournals.org).

[4] Self-reference_10: Fundamental Theory of Singularity; Formulated study – 1. [Volume 10, Issue 08, 2023]. (IJARPS –www.arcjournals.org).

[5] Self-reference_9: New Study of Gravitation in Singularity. [Volume 10, Issue 04, 2023]. (IJARPS – www.arcjournals.org)

[6] Self-reference_8: Fundamental Theory of Singularity. [Volume 10, Issue 03, 2023]. (IJARPS – www.arcjournals.org)

[7] Self-reference_7: Fourth dimension of space-time – Study of gravitation; part-2. [Volume 10, Issue 02, 2023]. (IJARPS – www.arcjournals.org)

[8] Self-reference_6: Fourth dimension of space-time – Study of gravitation; part-1. [Volume 10, Issue 01, 2023]. (IJARPS – www.arcjournals.org)

[9] Self-reference_5: Fundamental study of space-time – (Zero, One and Infinity). [Volume 10, Issue 01, 2023]. (IJARPS – www.arcjournals.org).

[10] Self-reference_4: Particle physics based on real dimensions of space-time. [Volume 9, Issue 10, 2022]. (IJARPS – www.arcjournals.org).

[11] Self-reference_3: General relativity Vs Quantum mechanics; Incompatibility solved with real dimensions of space-time. [Volume 9, Issue-9, 2022]. (IJARPS – www.arcjournals.org).

[12] Self-reference_2: Length contraction and time dilation are experimental but non-physical variations in space-time. [Volume-9, Issue-8, 2022]. (IJARPS – www.arcjournals.org).

[13] Self-reference_1: Length contraction and time dilation with real dimensions of space-time. [Volume-9, Issue-8, 2022]. (International Journal of Advanced Research in Physical Science (IJARPS – www.arcjournals.org).

AUTHOR'S BIOGRAPHY

Prabhakaran Natesan, Tamil Nadu, India. [shanatcop@gmail.com] Bachelor's degree in Electrical and Electronics Engineering (2011) – Affiliated to Anna University, Chennai.

"All the problems in the existence are already solved, means the solutions are always available in one of the Sp-ti frames. All that a man has to do is, just to put himself in the way that progresses towards the ultimate nature called nothing, in which everything that shows up is only for a time-being".

I see the fundamental theory of singularity and its application to arrive at the new theory of gravitation, to have evolved in time for which I just admitted myself as a medium to conduct the knowledge to flow through me to take its own course and evolve into the shape of a scripture. Only the time that decides when, where and how the secrets of space-time to be revealed to this world in some format picked up from its ever-living library. Otherwise, anyone trying to come up with these ideas to tell the people or open the secrets, which is not permitted by time, would disappear from this world itself without a trace. The work involves such a dying commitment that the efforts are blind and energy is spent in all the directions in darkness. The source and destination points being the one saved me to be still alive in this process. So, this very research work is evident for space-time to be finite… This proposed study is intended to be useful for education and subjected to reviews…

THANK YOU

www.ingramcontent.com/pod-product-compliance
Lightning Source LLC
Chambersburg PA
CBHW041334120726
48005CB00014B/2255